The Mass Explained

The Mass Explained

Thomas McMahon

CARILLON BOOKS

St. Paul, Minnesota

First published in Great Britain in 1977 by
MAYHEW-McCRIMMON
Great Wakering Essex England

Imprimatur: Christopher Creede, V.G.
July 1977

Carillon Books edition published December 1978

ISBN: 0-89310-041-2 hard
0-89310-042-0 paper
LC Card no: 78-059320
© 1977 Mayhew-McCrimmon

Printed in the United States of America

Contents

1 Why on Sunday?   1
2 From the Last Supper
   to Vatican II 27
3 The Mass Explained 45
4 Seasons of the Church 77
5 Art and Liturgy
   What to look for in a Church 97

TO THE PEOPLE OF STOCK, ESSEX,
I DEDICATE THIS BOOK

1

Why on Sunday?

I would like to begin this small book with what I consider to be one of the finest passages I have ever read on the Mass. It is by Dom Gregory Dix and from his book, *The Shape of the Liturgy.*

" 'Do this in memory of me' — was ever another command so obeyed? For century after century, spreading slowly to every continent and country and among every race on earth, this action has been done in every conceivable human circumstance for every conceivable human need, from infancy and before it, to extreme old age and after it, from the pinnacles of earthly greatness to the refuge of fugitives in the caves and dens of the earth. Men have found no better thing than this to do for Kings at their crowning and for criminals going to the scaffold; for armies in triumph or for a bride and bridegroom in a country church; for the proclamation of a dogma or for a good crop of wheat; for the wisdom of the parliament of a mighty nation or for a sick old woman afraid to die; for a schoolboy sitting an examination, or for Columbus setting out to discover America; for the famine of a whole province or for the soul of a dead lover; in thankfulness that a friend did not die of pneumonia; for the repentance of a sinner or for the settlement of a strike; while the lions roared at the nearby amphitheatre; on the beach at Dunkirk; while the hiss of scythes in the thick June grass came faintly through the windows of the church; tremulously, by an old monk on the fiftieth anniversary of his vows; furtively, by an exiled Bishop who had hewn timber all day in a prison camp — splendidly, for a canonisation — one could fill many pages with the reasons why men have done this, and not tell a hundredth part of them. And best of all, week by week, and month by month, on a hundred thousand successive Sundays, faithfully, unfailingly, across all the parishes of Christendom, priest and people continue to gather together in order to carry out this command 'Do this in memory of me!'

"To those who know a little of Christian history, probably the most moving of all the reflections it brings is not the thought of the great events and well-remembered saints, but of those innumerable millions of entirely obscure faithful men and women, every one with his or her own individual hopes and fears, joys and sorrows and loves — sins and temptations and prayers — once every bit as vivid and alive as mine are. They have left no slightest trace in this world, not even a name, but have passed to God, utterly forgotten by men. Yet each one of them believed and prayed as I believe and pray, and found it hard and grew slack and sinned and repented and fell again. Each of them worshipped at the Eucharist and found their thoughts wandering and tried again feeling heavy and unresponsive and yet knowing, just as really and pathetically as I do, these things.

"There is a little ill-spelled, ill-carved rustic epitaph of the fourth century from Asia Minor: 'Here sleeps the blessed Chione, who has found Jerusalem, for she prayed much.' Not another word is known of Chione, some peasant woman who lived in that vanished world of Christian Anatolia — but how lively if all that should survive after sixteen centuries were that one had prayed much, so that the neighbours who saw all one's life were sure one must have found Jerusalem! What did the Sunday Eucharist in her village church every week for a lifetime mean to the blessed Chione — and to the millions like her then, and every year since? The sheer stupendous quantity of the love of God which this ever repeated action has drawn from the obscure Christian multitudes through the centuries is in itself, an overwhelming thought."

In contrast to the above passage a woman said to me recently during a discussion on the Mass that the response she made with the most feeling and relief was the one at the end of Mass: "Thanks be to God!" Perhaps there have been occasions when we have all felt like that, and, yet how sad that it should be so. If we come along to our Sunday Mass not only out of a sense of duty but because it is Sunday, "The Lord's Day," when as Christians we celebrate his resurrection, then we come together as a community, in order to express our joy in song and prayer, to listen to God's word in the lessons and homily, and to celebrate the Eucharist together, then we should feel enormously uplifted and strengthened to go out and live our Christian lives. Our liturgy is something to be enjoyed. We speak about "celebrating" Mass and use such words as "celebrant" and "feast." All celebrations contain three elements (i) an event to celebrate; (ii) a gathering together in order to do it (we don't usually celebrate alone!); (iii) an action — we do something together. And so we gather together to celebrate the death and resurrection of Christ, through the Eucharistic action that he commanded us to do. This is our duty, but it is also something we should

3

delight in doing because of the joy and help that we receive.

If we come only out of a sense of duty, and are rather closed to participating or to being open and receptive toward the different parts of the Mass, then we may well be quite relieved when it is all over for another week! Not that I am putting all the blame on the person in the pew. The new Mass demands far more preparation on the part of all those involved — priest, readers, choir, servers and people. The whole effect depends upon each person doing his part carefully and well. And although, as I will mention later, we have a strict duty to worship God, if we reduce our reason for going to church to this alone it may engender a very negative approach. If, however, we come with a really positive approach and see how, in our worship, it is we who receive so much more from God than we could ever give to him, then our whole attitude will be different, and we will be much more open to receiving in the various ways that I now want to talk about.

1. The Christian Sunday

If you go into any town or village on a Sunday it looks completely different from any other day of the week. In deed, free from people and cars, it may be the only day to see what it really looks like! In his book, *The Meaning of Sunday*, J. A. Jungmann tells how every week Sunday transforms the area where we live, as business and industry close down. In our European civilization, which came from the spread of Christianity, we take this for granted, but it is in fact quite a remarkable phenomenon. We do not find anything quite like it in China, Japan, India or Africa and the reason is that it is something specifically and intrinsically Christian.

The old Sabbath celebrated the completion of God's

4

work of material creation, and commemorated the Covenant — when God brought his people out of slavery to freedom. In the book of Exodus we read, "Be sure that you observe the Sabbath day. It is a token between us, reminding you that I am the Lord and you are set apart for me." (Exodus 31.12.) To this day the pious Jewish family prepare everything for Saturday so that it may be a day of rest. Then at sunset on Friday they light the Sabbath candles and celebrate a meal similar to the Passover meal which Christ shared with his disciples, giving praise and thanks to God. Their Sabbath rest enables them to rejoice and give thanks to God who liberated them from "servile" labor and brought them to freedom. The chief memorial of the liberation is in the Passover meal.

Although our Sunday is not just a continuation of the Jewish Sabbath, they have several things in common. We too have been liberated. Christ by his death and resurrection freed us from slavery to sin and won us the freedom of being sons of God. And so a new kind of creation has begun — not in the material order of the world and the body, but in the spiritual order, the soul. The Sabbath celebrated creation in the order of nature, whereas our Sunday celebrates creation in the order of grace.

Both Sabbath and Sunday are memorials of a Covenant, i.e., the agreement by which we are all in different ways brought from slavery to freedom. Both memorials are celebrated in a meal, the Old Covenant in the Passover meal and the New Covenant in the Mass. To show that it was a "new and everlasting Covenant" which had replaced the "old," Christians celebrated the day on which this had happened, i.e., Easter Sunday. To observe this each week they changed their weekly Sabbath to Sunday. It has been known by various names, all of which gave some indication of its special meaning.

First of all, there was the name by which we know it

5

now, "SUNDAY." This has its origin in the oriental worship of the sun, which was widespread in the East before the time of our Lord. It had been introduced into the Roman empire toward the end of the third century and was to be the last of the great pagan religions of the Roman world. It comes as a surprise to many to know that our Lord was probably not born on December 25th! This day was an important pagan feast on which they celebrated the birth of the sun. Christians retained it, but instead celebrated the birth of the Sun of Justice, Jesus Christ. Although the word Sunday has this pagan origin, the symbol of the sun would seem very appropriate to describe the day on which we celebrate each week the resurrection. As St. Jerome says, "The Lord created all the days of the week, and the ordinary weekdays could be the days of the Jews, or of heretics, or of the heathen; but the Lord's day, the day of the resurrection, the day of the Christians, is our own. And if the heathen call it 'dies solis,' we are quite ready to accept this description too, for on this day the light appeared, on this day the Sun of Righteousness shone forth."

As we know from early accounts, this day was also called "THE FIRST DAY." To break bread on "the first day of the week" had special significance, since it was on this day, Easter Sunday, that they discovered the empty tomb. On the first day of the week also Christ appeared to his disciples at Emmaus and broke bread with them. Many of his apppearances are recorded as being "on the first day of the week . . .". By tradition it has always been held that it was also on this day that he ascended back to the Father, and it was on this day that he sent down the Holy Spirit on our Lady and the disciples. All of this made it "the Lord's day" in a very special way.

This name, "THE LORD'S DAY," was quite common in post-apostolic times and is referred to by St. John. It derives from the fact that after undergoing death on the cross, Christ rose again on Easter Sunday and proved himself to be the Lord. "The Lord's day" is still used in many countries. In Greek the word is "Kyriake" (which you will recognize from the Kyrie of the mass as meaning "Lord") and in Latin it is "dominica" (from dominus, the Lord). In French this day of the week is known as "dimanche," in Italian "domenica" and in Spanish "domingo." The Byzantine Christians and the Russian people still call it "resurrection day."

Our last name for this day is "THE EIGHTH DAY." This may seem curious when it was also known as "the first day"! Let me explain. God had created the world in six days and rested on the seventh. On a Sunday, i.e., the eighth day, he took up his work once more and brought it to perfection with a new creation, the spiritual creation in the order of grace. In this sense Sunday is not the beginning but the fulfilment of the week, since material creation only leads up to spiritual creation. Hence the number eight came to represent Christ's new life as he rose again. We read in the epistle of Barnabas, ". . . we also celebrate with gladness the eighth day on which Jesus rose from the dead, and was made manifest, and ascended into heaven" (15.8). To the same effect St. Ambrose declared, "He, by his resurrection, sanctified the eighth day; it began likewise to be the first, that is the eighth, the eighth, that is the first." It was referred to in this way by the second Vatican council in its constitution on the sacred liturgy which said, "By apostolic tradition which took its origin from the very day of Christ's resurrection, the Church celebrates the Paschal mystery every eighth day." Since in the sacrament of baptism this new re-creation begins, and we too begin to die to sin and share the new risen life of Christ, baptismal fonts often had eight sides as a way of expressing this same idea.

Sunday then, as we can see from all these names, is something very special: a day of new beginning and new life. It should be a day of deep gladness and spiritual joy. We should echo in our hearts the words of the psalmist, "This day was made by the Lord; we rejoice and are glad" (Psalm 117).

2. We Come Together as a Community

One of the problems created by modern travel is that we all belong to a series of different communities. Up to a hundred and fifty years ago everything centered around the local community. To-day the world is a very small place. It is often enriching to go outside one's own community and to be able to receive and give in a kind of mutual exchange. On the other hand, the local life of the area we live in can be impoverished if we are constantly going outside of it and take no real part in it.

By his very nature man is meant to live in community rather than in isolation: we are born into a family, and belong at the same time to God's family through baptism, and to the larger family of mankind. It is necessary to remind ourselves that the word "church" means first and foremost not a building (indeed, no building as such existed for the first three centuries, until after the persecutions) but a community of people who are learning to love and grow together in the way Christ showed us. What John Donne wrote in his poem, *The Bell,* three hundred years ago is true to-day: "Any man's death diminishes me, since I am involved in the whole of humanity; and therefore do not seek to know for whom the bell tolls, because it tolls for thee."

If we read the Acts of the Apostles, we see how the early Christians had a wonderful sense of community and how their love of Christ led them to share and care for each other. "The faithful all lived together and owned every-thing in common; they sold their goods and possessions and shared out the proceeds among themselves according to each one's need. They went as a body to the Temple every day, but met in their homes for the breaking of bread, they shared their food gladly and generously." (Acts 2:44-47).

They worshipped together, and from their worship came their love and concern for one another. So should it be for us. Coming together for worship should be the main pur-pose of our community, and out of this should arise our care for one another. The Church is made visible as it comes together around its Bishop or priest, in a communal celebration of the liturgy. We are primarily and essentially a worshipping community and nothing in the whole life of the parish is more important than the Sunday Mass.

Yet, in worship, there is still strong resistance on the part of the people to the notion that they are a community, and people at church still tend to regard themselves as isolated individuals. Most churches tend to fill up from the back, and even when a church is fairly empty, individuals will be scattered around rather than come together! At Mass the liturgical assembly is a community of faith, of which the recitation of the creed is the most obvious expression. It is also a community of love, of which the Eucharist is the sign. Union as a liturgical community is expressed in the hearing of God's world, in common prayer and song, in the common offering of the sacrifice and in the sharing at the Lord's table.

Many large and splendid churches were built in the Mid-dle Ages not only because of civic pride but because all would assemble together for the one service. To-day our churches are used several times on a Sunday with a mul-tiplication of Masses. But the Church still recognizes the ideal of the one celebration and has retained this on important occasions such as the one mass of the Lord's Supper on Maundy Thursday and the Paschal Vigil at Easter.

To "celebrate" Mass implies coming together with others of a like mind. A meal unites people; an invitation is a sign of friendship. United in the common action of eating and drinking together, we strengthen the bonds of friendship. So in the Mass, "May all who share this one bread and one cup become one body in Christ" (Eucharistic prayer IV). So the people of an area who are scattered during the week about their different tasks come together as one family on Sunday to worship God.

Having celebrated together, the christian Community learns to love the world with Christ's love. From its liturgical celebration it should turn outwards to the world: conscious of all that goes on in it, suffering when it suffers and helping when it can. A real community will embrace and support all kinds of people — the mature and the immature, the misfits and the well-adjusted, the unloved and the emotionally crippled. At the beginning the followers of Christ were not called Christians, but they so practised the teaching of Christ in their lives that people gave them this name. As St. Paul reminds us in the twelfth chapter to the Corinthians, we have all received different gifts in order to render different services within the community.

In a family the joy or sorrow of one is the joy or the sorrow of all. St. Paul reminds us, "You should bear each other's burdens and so fulfil the law of Christ." We must be alive to the fact that life is a family affair in which we all help. To love and to open ourselves to others is to allow ourselves to be committed. It also makes us vulnerable to being hurt and rejected. Real life is in community and not in isolation. We must discover the human needs of the communities in which we live and relate the gospel of Christ directly to them.

The kingdom of God is a kingdom of peace, and it must be demonstrated in visible terms that the christian gospel is able to break down all those barriers which divide people and create destructive tension. St. Paul admonishes the people of Galatia — ". . . not to go snapping at each other and tearing each other to pieces, you had better watch or you will destroy the whole community." True strength comes from unity and division only results in weakness. In the book, *Watership Down,* the rabbits all bind together in adversity and in their search for a new home. The chief rabbit warns them: "Rabbits have enough enemies as it is — they ought not to make more among themselves."

Finally, any Christian community should be the center of celebration and joy: the Christian believes he has discovered the source of true joy. All our actions and attitudes should reflect something of the joy of the gospel and love of life in the kingdom of God.

3. We express our joy in prayer and song

In the epistle of St. James we read, "Is one of you unhappy? Let him fall to prayer. Is one of you cheerful? For him a psalm." (James 5:13). I hope we don't come to pray just when we are unhappy! But it is true that it tends to be at the time when things are troubling us that we turn to God in prayer. In the Mass we find all forms of prayer — repentance (at the beginning), praise (Glory to God in the highest), petition (in the collect), intercession (the offertory) and thanksgiving (the Eucharistic prayer). It is above all community prayer; but in the moments of silence there is also a time for private prayer.

Singing is very important in the Mass for various reasons. First of all, it expresses our joy. It is natural to sing when we are happy, and we should be especially happy to sing the praises of God. St. Paul wrote to the Ephesians, "Let your contentment be in the Holy Spirit; your tongues unloosed in psalms and hymns and spiritual music as you sing and give praise to the Lord in your hearts." (Ephesians 5:19). Singing is a natural human expression not only of joy but also of sadness, love, and worship. All the arts explain the mysteries of religion, and especially music which can transcend this world and put men in touch with God. European music sprang from Christianity and most of its early development depended upon ecclesiastical patronage. Singing is praise. Singing reflects God's glory. Pope John said, "The Spirit of God is the soul of music."

The church's music is rooted in Jewish and oriental chant, some of which was in use before the birth of Christ. When the Church gained her freedom, a choral chant began in Rome and a school of chanters was formed which received its final form from Pope Gregory the Great at the end of the sixth century and is the chant we know as Gregorian. It is a tremendous achievement in the field of unaccompanied music. The Church's music then developed through plainsong and polyphony to the music of Mozart, and in more recent times to composers like Britten and Berkeley. This tradition is unique and it not only enshrines nearly two thousand years of spirituality and mysticism but also has had a profound influence on the development of secular music.

The oldest religious songs still in use are the psalms, many of them written three thousand years ago. "Sing to the Lord a new song. . . . Praise him with trumpet sound, with lute, pipe and dance, praise him with loud clashing cymbals." (Psalm 150). The psalms were written in Hebrew and there are one hundred and fifty of them. King David composed many of them and he is known as "the singer of the songs of Israel." They have been prayed and sung by the Jews in their worship; by Christ and the apostles; by the Church at Mass; and by monks and nuns in their Divine Office all down the centuries. They are written in the Eastern style of those days, full of concrete images, describing God as a Shepherd or a Rock, comparing the upright man to a tree planted beside flowing waters. If the psalmist sometimes seems very unforgiving toward his enemies, then remember that he was writing long before the birth of Christ! There are two great themes, God and man, and man on his journey to God with shouts of joy, praise, sorrow, anger, thanksgiving and despair. In this sense the psalmist speaks as our contemporary, since whatever mood we experience he has felt it before us and expressed it in a psalm. The psalms were meant to be sung, with the accompaniment of a stringed instrument. One of the advantages of having the Mass in the vernacular is that the psalms, until now sung or recited mainly by priests and nuns, may now be sung and prayed by everybody.

Why is it the singing in many Catholic parishes is so poor? I don't believe Catholics are less joyful than other Christians nor that they have less ability to sing! I think it is because, with a silent Latin Mass, or one sung partly by choir and people, we have little tradition of congregational singing. It is now slowly being built up. Here in our country parish, the people sing with great enthusiasm and the choir like to stay on after Sunday Mass to learn new hymns and descants! It is true to say that the effectiveness of a Mass with music depends very largely on the response of the people. As the council document on Sacred Music says: "Liturgical action is given a more noble form when sacred rites are solemnized in song, with the assistance of sacred ministers and the active participation of the people." (113) But there is very much a place for a choir in every church, to lead the singing and to provide the occasional part-singing or anthem. The choir will keep alive what is best in traditional church music as well as learning new settings.

If the Mass is meant to be a celebration, then let us express our joy in song. Here is something really to celebrate! Christ has borne our sorrows and our sins, he has come to set us free. Even if things are hard for us personally, we find hope in the risen Lord and in the promise he brings us.

The second reason why singing is a really integral part of the Mass is that certain liturgical texts are definitely written to be sung rather than recited. Think of the "Glory be to God on high," the "Alleluia," the "Sanctus" or the acclamation after the Consecration — how much better both the meaning and mood are expressed when they are sung. It is much the same with a heartfelt "Kyrie" or "Agnus Dei."

Lastly, singing binds us together. If the entrance hymn at the beginning is one people know well, then it helps to draw us all together at the beginning of the Mass as "una voce" — with one voice, we prepare to worship God.

4. We listen to God's Word

It was not for nothing that St. Peter began his first proclamation of the Good News on Pentecost Sunday with the words: "Listen to me." (Acts 2:14). Listening to another person isn't always easy, maybe because we have made up our minds already and are quite closed to listening to anything or anyone else; or maybe prejudices get in the way. We are not always prepared to accept the consequences of what we hear, so we may prefer not to give our attention. Really to listen to somebody requires sympathy and humility. It means trying to understand. Real listening is an act of love, a sort of hospitality. It gives welcome to another human being. And if we want to hear the Spirit, we have to let go of everything else, and be truly open to the Word. The psalmist calls upon us: "O that today you would listen to his voice, harden not your hearts." (Psalm 94). As we sit down in church let us prepare like the infant Samuel to open our hearts and say "Speak Lord, your servant listens." (I Samuel 3:10).

If listening is hard anyway, it can be specially hard in church! There may be a lot of noise; the reader may be unclear and it may be a complicated lesson. Sometimes there will be missalettes in order to help the concentration. Ideally speaking, when we have good readers and good acoustics, these should not be necessary. We should be able to direct our attention to the center of action. During the readings we must try hard to do two things: to listen to God's message with attention and respect, recognizing it for what it is; and to discern its message for our lives.

We must have a strong realization that the Bible is God himself speaking to us. He reveals himself to us in the great truths he wants us to know and tells us of our responsibility to him. God approaches man through word and deed, seeking his response by faith. It has come to us through others: "In many and various ways he spoke of old to our fathers by the prophets." (Heb. 1:1). Finally God has spoken to us through his Son who became incarnate. "The Word was made flesh." A word is an expression of a thought; so the Word reveals God to us. Although this Word of God has come down through the centuries it is "ever old yet ever new," as the writer of the hymn puts it: "I believe what God has spoken, through his Church whose word is true. Boldly she proclaims his gospel — ever old yet ever new."

This brings me to the second point: how we listen for a purpose and what our response should be. You see, the

Word of God cannot be read or listened to as if it were something that belonged to the past. It is a living Word, addressed to us here and now in the present, making demands of us, since God asks of us not only our minds but also our hearts. It is meant to have an immediate bearing upon our lives and summons us to a present decision. It is an invitation saving those who accept and judging those who refuse. "Be ye doers of the Word, not hearers only." (James 1:17). The Word in readings, chants and prayers is addressed to men in order to evoke a response. The arrangement of the liturgy during the first part of the Mass shows this. The three readings and the homily are the proclamation of the Word; the psalm, the creed and the prayers of the faithful are our response to the Word. But above all, we respond to the Word by living it. Isaiah said: "As the rain and snow come down and water the earth, and make it yield and give growth to provide seed for the sower and bread for eating, so the word that goes from my mouth does not return empty." In the Gospels our Lady would be an example of someone who pondered on the Word in her heart and accepted it by a personal response, while the rich young man found the demands of the Gospel too much and walked away.

We have just celebrated the quincentenary of William Caxton who founded the first printing press in this country in the precincts of Westminster Abbey. We can reflect on the power of words during those five hundred years, and how through them the ideologies of people long since dead continue to influence us. In this way also the Word of God has penetrated and shaped countless lives. As St. Paul said, "The Word of God is something alive and active: it cuts like any double-edged sword but more finely: it can slip through the place where the soul is divided from the spirit, or joints from the marrow: it can judge the secret emotions and thoughts. No created thing can hide from him; everything is uncovered and open to the eyes of the one to whom we must give an account of ourselves." (Heb. 4:12,13). The Word of God informs, invites, pleads, demands and condemns. It makes an appeal to all men regardless of their condition, and they cannot escape it. This is also expressed in psalm 138: "O where can I go from your spirit, where can I flee from your face? If I climb the mountains you are there. If I lie in the grave you are there."

The readings and homily at Mass serve one ultimate purpose, to draw us all, mind and heart, into the very presence of God who is speaking to us. We must listen and respond to the Word by giving ourselves to it so completely that we become it in our lives. To the extent to which we become it, we are its proclamation to the world.

5. We Celebrate the Eucharist

Elsewhere in this book, I have explained what we are doing in the whole of the Eucharistic prayer, as we make present once again the act of Christ's salvation. In this section I want to speak about the fruit of this mystery — Holy Communion — what it really means and how our participation in the Mass is only fully realized by our receiving Communion, and what a help it should be in our lives.

(a) Holy Communion is faith in the presence of the risen Christ.

Rather like the different names that were given to "the Lord's Day," mentioned above, the various names by which Communion was known give us an idea of its essence and intrinsic meaning. One of these names used by St. Paul is "The Lord's Supper." This places the whole meal aspect in the foreground and this has always been a particularly strong element. Many signs of the Old Testament foreshadowed events of the New Testament which were to be their fulfilment. For example there was water. In a dry land water above all else symbolized life. So in Baptism it became the symbol of the new life we would share in being baptized into Christ.

And so with bread. God, in a special way, often fed the people of the Old Testament when they were on a journey. We read how Elijah wanted to give up, when God renewed him by food: "Get up and eat, or the journey will be too long for you." (I Kings 19:7). In the same way God nourished the people with manna on their journey through the desert to the promised land. This was a sign of what he was to do for us. But for us, it was to be something more ". . . it is not as it was with your fathers, who ate manna and died none the less; the man who eats this bread will live eternally." (John 6:59). Jesus tried to prepare the people by the miracle of the feeding of the five thousand with five loaves and two fishes. The similarity was striking as Jesus said grace over the bread, "Then Jesus took the loaves and gave thanks . . ." (John 6:11).

The real explanation of what it is all about comes only a little later in the same chapter of St. John. "I am the bread of life. He who comes to me will never be hungry; he who believes in me will never be thirsty." (John 6:35). The Jews couldn't understand or accept this and so they fell to disputing with one another, "How can this man give us his flesh to eat?" Jesus assured them in this way, "I tell you solemnly, if you do not eat of the flesh of the Son of Man and drink his blood you will not have life in you. Anyone who does eat of my flesh and drinks my blood has eternal life, and I shall raise him up on the last day. For my flesh is real food and by blood is real drink. He who eats my flesh and drinks my blood lives in me and I in him. As I, who am sent by the living Father, myself draw life from the Father so whoever eats me will draw life

18

from me. This is the bread come down from heaven; not like the bread our ancestors ate; they are dead, but anyone who eats this bread will live forever." (John 6:55-58).

Seemingly this did not help very much, since we then find his followers saying, "This is intolerable language. How can we accept it?" After this incident we find that many of his disciples left him. Almost despondent, Christ turns to his apostle and says: "What about you, do you want to go away too?" And the wonderful words of St. Peter: "Lord, who shall we go to? You have the message of eternal life, and we believe." (John 6:67-68).

It is the last response, one of faith, that we too have to make in the Eucharist. We may not find it any easier than the disciples did — and yet it is not irrational or unreasonable faith, because it is based on God's word and on the many signs He has given us.

We all hunger for the bread of life. In our Western world where there is plenty to eat and a high standard of living, most of us have everything we need. And yet, are we satisfied? The hungry are not only to be found in the third world. When Mother Teresa came over to this country, she remarked about the great affluence she found in our material society, but said that unfortunately this had led to great poverty of spirit.

Modern man has a terrible need for a satisfaction of spiritual hunger which the materialistic, technological culture we have created cannot satisfy. Hunger can be found in the well-nourished homes of our great urban concourses — not just for material things, but for the ultimate. We hunger for truth, goodness, happiness, lasting peace. Once again the reason was given by Our Lord in this same passage, "It is the spirit that gives life, the flesh has nothing to offer." (John 6:63). And as in life, ". . . man cannot live by bread alone," (Matthew 4) — but hungers for deeper things, so in the Eucharist, we must see it as something more than just food to sustain and nourish the soul. We must go beyond that and see with the eyes of faith the presence of the risen Christ. Thus can we say with the disciples at Emmaus on the first Easter Sunday, "we recognised him in the breaking of bread." (Lk. 24:35).

(b) Holy Communion is the means of union with God and with one another.

In an earlier section I have spoken about community and said how difficult it is to bind individuals together as a real community. Although singing and other actions done together can be a help, the main action that causes us to come together and through which we deepen our union with God and one another, is the Communion. Its very name implies this and we see this more clearly if we think of a family celebration at Christmas time, or on the occasion of a wedding. We come together so that people may share in the joy of the occasion, and what is provided to eat and drink is a means of furthering that fellowship.

In the Old Testament it was through taking part in the Passover meal that one identified oneself with the people of God. Christ often compared the heavenly kingdom to a great banquet or wedding feast as in Matthew 22:1-10. This is not because we will be concerned in heaven with eating and drinking (hopefully, heavenly bodies won't require that!) but it expresses the idea of a family, a real community gathered together in joy and celebration and eternal blessedness. A communication of relationships is built into the very idea of eating and drinking. We share it with others. Therefore the "meal setting" of the Last Supper tells us something of its purpose.

Union implies sharing — at the Last Supper and since that time, whenever the words of Christ are said, we share in his redemptive work. Although the bonds of human love are very great, this is something greater still, since in the words of St. Augustine, "We are assimilated into

Christ." It is the parable of the vine and the branches. St. Paul describes it by telling us to "put on" the Lord Jesus Christ, i.e., identify with him in attitudes of mind and heart. When we eat with someone, we identify with them to some extent — we invite our friends to a meal in order to deepen our friendship. This is why the Pharisees protested when Christ went to eat in the homes of sinners.

Perhaps he wanted to show us also that eating with someone not only is a sign of unity, but it effects unity — it brings it about. It heals and unites and deepens friendship and this is the mission of Christ. St. Luke inserted in the narrative of the Lord's Supper, a passage on unity which Matthew had placed elsewhere — and indication of the theology of unity that Luke saw therein.

John went still further and put in the washing of the feet, a rite of hospitality and charity.

Happily, Communion under both kinds is now possible on many occasions. For twelve hundred years all received under both kinds but this practice died out, partly for theological reasons, (Christ is wholly present under either kind alone) and partly for practical reasons, in case of an accident. In receiving both the bread and the wine the sign is more expressive and complete and fulfils Our Lord's words when he said, "take this, all of you, and drink from it. . . ."

Holy Communion is a foretaste of the heavenly banquet, "Happy are those who are called to his supper." The people come up together to receive the body and blood of Christ, and in doing so they are united even more closely with Christ and with one another. It is this above all that will transform us from being a gathering of individuals to being a community.

We establish a relationship with one another and through eating and drinking together express a loving and trusting unity; therefore our willingness to share and serve what we have received is a pledge of future glory to come — "He who eats this bread shall live for ever." (John 6:51).

The Messianic banquet means the kingdom will be made up of a community with God. Through Holy Communion we can begin to do this already here on earth.

The Sunday observance

I have tried to show in these five short sections how much our Sunday Mass should be a really joyful and helpful celebration in which we feel a need to take part, rather than a mere duty. Duty is a word not much in favor these days and yet there must always be a profound sense in which to worship God remains the foremost duty of mankind.

If we think about it we see how all relationships in life bring with them certain joys and certain responsibilities. If we think of the relationship between parents and children we can see this. It is the same with God. He is Our Father both through creation (when He gave life to the body) and through baptism (when He gave life to the soul). Just as parents and children should not go through life ignoring one another but deepening their relationship, so we should not forget our heavenly Father. It would be sad if parents and children sustained their relationship out of a sense of duty alone and not out of love. So it is with God — we may come to church out of a sense of duty, but how much better if we come because of the love we have for God and the need we feel for Him.

If we come with this attitude of love, we will already have opened our hearts to sharing and receiving in all the ways I have mentioned. We may not always feel like attending church! Quite often one hears people say, "You should only go when you feel like it, — at Christmas for

22

example." This is reducing it to a purely emotional approach, and we have only to ask ourselves whether or not we would apply this approach to our work or to any other responsible task in life. We know only too well that we cannot always follow our feelings in life and allow the heart to govern our head. Our feelings change and we cannot base responsible decisions just on the mood of the moment but on what we think and know to be right.

Whether we are happy, sorrowful, in pain or whatever, we should always be aware of our need for God and express it in worship. Also, we must never underestimate in life the power of things to change us once we are caught up in them. How often we start something we don't feel like doing only to end up enjoying it and feeling quite different. Whatever our mood of the moment, God knows us better than we know ourselves. As St. Augustine said "He is nearer to us than we are to ourselves."

We have reason to be thankful that our church-going is confirmed by a Church precept, since it helps our frail human nature in this observance. The existence of this obligation does not mean that we do not come without love. Human nature is weak and we often need the law to support us in our weakness. We must beware on the other hand not to measure the faith of others by their frequency in going to church.

What is to be done when adolescents refuse to go to Mass on Sunday? I think one should let young people see that one treats the matter very seriously, though not fanatically. At the same time, faith in Christ is free and cannot be forced. Gradually the young people should be allowed responsibility for their own Mass going, so that they feel a certain independence in their own decision. They may prefer one Mass to another, to go with the family or on their own. This will help to prepare them for the time when they will leave home.

From the very beginning, attendance at the Sunday Eucharist was regarded as a criterion of faithfulness among Christians. It was not until the middle of the fourth century that we read, "if a layman has not taken part for three weeks in the Sunday worship of the community in which he lives, he is to be excluded from the church." It is interesting to note that for them, the greatest punishment of all was this exclusion from the community and the Eucharist. They drew all their inspiration from the Mass. There were no schools of Bible classes in those days — the church had just emerged from three centuries of persecution. And yet this was the very period when the pagan philosophy of life was to be superceded by a Christian philosophy which finally produced the Christian culture of the Middle Ages. And when we look for visible and human factors to which we can ascribe this amazing transformation, we can find none other than the liturgy of the church, especially the Sunday Mass.

Speaking about Sunday, the Vatican Council in its document on the liturgy said, "The Lord's Day is therefore the primordial feast day which is proposed to, and imposed upon the piety of the faithful so that it may become a day of joy and of rest from work." The term "servile work" was used in earlier times to define what work was to be avoided on Sunday in order to preserve its proper character. Servile work meant hard manual labor. We may not find the word very appealing but we must remember what social protection it signified for slaves and manual workers. Thus the church prevented their working one day a week.

In England the emphasis has changed noticeably over the past hundred years. Whereas in Victorian times more people went to church on a Sunday, it would seem that joy wasn't very much in evidence. At one period all forms of recreation, even going for a walk, were forbidden! To-day it is the reverse; fewer people go to church, but are quite determined to enjoy the weekend by "getting away from it all"!

Sunday rest is meant to give us time for God and time to re-create ourselves, by reading, reflecting, discussing or whatever makes us think more deeply about the meaning of life. It is a time for family and friends. It is a day when a couple can spend more time in each other's company and with their children. In our busy world this is increasingly necessary and enriches our lives with a quiet strength which can in turn help us in the days that follow.

Sunday is the "Day of the Lord" and so belongs to God and we must worship Him. Let us have a real awareness of what it is we are celebrating and so welcome the day as one of rejoicing, sharing, receiving, as well as giving to God. In the words of Fr. Clifford Howell — "it is a day of real recreation."

This worship should be at the center of our work and of our lives. In the pattern of the medieval village the houses and workshops were built around the church, to show that God should be the center of our lives. The church steeple stood out and pointed to the sky and still serves to direct our minds "to things that are above." All worship is for the glory of God and sanctification of man. Let us come along full of joy to give to God the glory that is His due.

At the same time may we ourselves find the means of holiness and strength in coming together as a community — in lifting up our hearts in song and prayer — in listening to God's word and in celebrating the Eucharist.

Then we shall find ourselves echoing in our hearts the Psalmist's words: "This day was made by the Lord, we rejoice and are glad." (Psalm 117).

2

From the Last Supper to
Vatican II

1. The Last Supper

The first Mass was, of course, on Maundy Thursday.
Our knowledge of what this was like comes from two
sources — from the accounts we have in the Gospels of
the Last Supper, and from what we know of the Jewish
Passover meal. Essentially it is the Paschal meal with the
Last Supper words of Our Lord at the time of eating the
bread and drinking the cup.

The Paschal meal had quite a lot of ritual surrounding
it. Before the meal proper, bitter herbs and unleavened
bread were served with a cup of wine. This frugal diet
recalled the hunger experienced by the people during their
journey out of Egypt. Then the son or youngest member of
the family would ask what this meant. The father of the

house with a prayer of thanksgiving to God then told the account of their liberation from bondage in Egypt. This ended with the singing of psalms 112 and 113, during which the people answered "Alleluia."

After this the meal proper began. The father of the house took some of the unleavened bread, broke it, said a blessing over it and passed it around. This was a sign of their brotherly Communion in the one bread and it marked the beginning of the meal. It was over this bread that Our Lord said, "This is my body, which is given up for you." Then the Paschal Lamb was eaten.

When the meal was over, again the father of the house took the cup filled with wine, raised it up slightly while he said the grace after the meal and then all drank from it, and recited psalms 113 and 135. It was at this point that Our Lord said, "This is my blood of the new and everlasting Covenant."

We can see clearly the pattern of the Last Supper. The consecration of the bread is connected with the blessing before the eating of the lamb, signifying "common-union" or "Communion," and the consecration of the chalice is connected with the grace after the meal.

2. Mass of the Apostles

Our Lord ended the Last Supper by saying, "Do this in memory of me." How was this to be carried out? A full account of the early Mass has come down to us from the year 150. Before that date we have only slight glimpses and hints. We do have various references in the Gospels and three references in the Acts of the Apostles.

First of all, we know that the celebration was separated from the Jewish rite of Passover partly because of all the ceremonial surrounding it but also because the Paschal celebration was restricted by law to once a year.

At an early date they brought together the two consecrations. In the Paschal meal there was a gap between the two: "When supper was ended he took the cup. . . .", but, in the account by Matthew and Mark, the two consecrations are already together. One clue is the name by which this new event was known: "The breaking of bread." They still joined in worship at the Temple in order to pray and listen to the Scriptures, but then followed it by something new which only Christians did, "continuing daily with one accord in the Temple . . . and breaking bread in their homes." (Acts 2:46).

There is a delightful account in a later chapter when they came together one Sunday evening at Troas, ". . . for the breaking of bread." (Acts 20:7), and St. Paul preached a very long sermon which went on until midnight. During the sermon a young man sitting on the window-sill fell asleep and so fell out of the window from the third floor to the ground, and died! Happily St. Paul brought him back to life again.

Although one cannot be certain, it would appear that this early Mass was usually in the context of a meal, which would be combined with the memorial meal and the essential sacramental rite which Christ had conferred upon it. For them a meal was always a religious occasion and this would make it especially so. The Corinthians certainly combined it with a meal. When on one occasion they had eaten and drunk too much, St. Paul admonished them that they were not in a fit state for the sacramental part of the meal: "He is eating and drinking damnation to himself if he eats and drinks unworthily, not recognising the Lord's body for what it is." (I Cor. 11:29).

Therefore the elements that composed this early Mass

would include (a) a meal setting, (b) the grace and prayer of Thanksgiving, introduced by the invitation which we still have before the preface, "Lift up your hearts . . . let us give thanks to the Lord our God," (c) the two consecrations.

Gradually, the meal setting was abandoned and this came about in two ways. First, the prayer of thanksgiving in this new Christian assembly was no longer just one of thanksgiving for the gifts of food and drink, but one which recalled the goodness of God in all his gifts and especially in redeeming us. Secondly, the gathering had grown too large for domestic table-gatherings in the home. Thus the meal character fell out and the Eucharistic celebration alone remained. This required only one table for the celebrant, leaving room for all the people. There would be only one Eucharistic celebration in each congregation.

Up to this time it had been the Jewish custom to hold these meals in the evening, but now that the meal had been separated from the holy Eucharist the people could meet at any time. Thereafter the custom grew of meeting early in the morning on Sunday. As they greeted the rising sun they thought of the risen Christ. An early hour was more convenient since they would then avoid notice. Gradually the tie with the Temple was broken, and after the break with the Synagogue and the persecutions in the year 44, the Scripture readings were added before the Eucharist — and so the Mass pattern began to evolve.

3. First full account of the Mass in the year 150 by St. Justin

St. Justin, philosopher, martyr and layman in Rome, wrote this first full double account of the Mass which followed Christian Baptism. "After we have baptised him who professes our belief and associates with us, we lead him into the assembly of those called the Brethren and there say prayers in common for ourselves, for the newly-baptised and for all others all over the world. After the prayers we greet one another with a holy kiss. Then bread and a cup of water and wine mixed are brought to the one presiding over the brethren. He takes it, gives praise and glory to the Father of all in the name of the Son and of the Holy Ghost and gives thanks at length for the gifts that we were worthy to receive from him. When he has finished the prayers and thanksgiving, the whole crowd standing by cries out in agreement, 'Amen.' 'Amen,' is a Hebrew word meaning 'So may it be.'

"After the presiding official has said thanks and the people have joined with him, the Deacons, as they are styled by us, distribute as food for all those present the bread and the wine mixed with water over which thanks had been offered. These also are carried to those not present. This food is known amongst us as the Eucharist. No one may partake of it unless he is convinced of the truth of our teaching and is cleansed in the bath of Baptism.

"And on that day which is called after the Sun, all who are in the town and in the country gather together for a communal celebration . . . and the memoirs of the Apostles or the writings of the Prophets are read as long as time permits. After the reader has finished his task, the presiding official gives an address, urgently admonishing his hearers to practice these beautiful teachings in their lives. Then all stand up together and recite prayers. Following the prayers as has been shown above, the bread and wine are brought and the one presiding offers up prayers and thanks, as much as in him lies. The people chime in with 'Amen.' Then takes place the distribution to all attending of the things over which the thanksgiving has been spoken. The Deacons bring a portion to the absent. Besides those who are well-to-do give whatever they will. All that is gathered is deposited with the one presiding, who therewith helps orphans and widows. . . ."

In this account there is great emphasis on "giving thanks," and hence the name "Eucharist" from the Greek which means "to give thanks." There is a sense of oneness between priest and people, and their loud cry "Amen" at the end of the Eucharistic prayer puts their seal on all the priest does. Together with the prayer of thanksgiving there is present at this time, though not so clearly expressed, the idea of sacrifice for the purpose of rendering thanks.

The Mass of the first three centuries was still very flexible. There was a unified order and a set framework, but for many of the prayer-texts the priest was allowed to use his own words. However, the actual design of the great Eucharistic prayer of thanksgiving was always the same, beginning with the short dialogue, as we have before the Preface, and ending with the great Amen. And so emerges a liturgy with a certain unity and structure, and yet with flexibility. We already find these elements:

1. Lessons taken from the Apostles.
2. Sermon following on the readings.
3. Prayers of intercession.
4. The kiss of peace.
5. The Eucharistic prayer — a prayer of thanksgiving and praise.
6. Communion under both kinds for all.
7. A collection of money for the poor.

The priest used the language of the people and wore no special clothes when celebrating. The vestments he wears now were the ordinary clothes of those days. The ordinary meal or agape which they had before communion was discontinued, since occasional abuses had crept in such as over-eating and over-drinking, and also the number of those present at Mass had greatly increased.

4. Mass in the Fourth Century

(a) In the East.

In his great tome, *Mass of the Roman Rite*, Jungmann, describes how within the Greek territory of the Eastern end of the Mediterranean at this time certain areas began to dominate, such as Alexandria and Antioch. Particular liturgies spread from these centers, together with stricter control of worship. More and more of the text was set down in writing. We do have a Mass from this period, and it begins with readings from Scripture, a homily, prayers of intercession and a benediction. Then follows the Eucharistic prayer, beginning with: "Fit it is and proper to praise, to glorify and to exalt thee, the everlasting Father of the only-begotten, Jesus Christ." The end of the prayer mentions the angels of God and ends with the familiar: "Holy, holy, holy Lord of Sabaoth, heaven and earth are full of his glory."

There was also a greater emphasis upon sacrificial worship. At the time of St. Basil, in the late fourth century, there was a growing consciousness of sin and increasing reverence which led to fewer people receiving Holy Communion. This was probably the result of Arianism (Arius denied the divinity of Christ and his views were condemned at the Council of Nicea), leading to a renewed emphasis being put by the Church on Christ's divinity. The awe and reverence is discernible right through to the Middle Ages, where man was all too conscious of himself as a sinner and saw God as his judge. This gave rise to such chants as the "Dies irae" (Day of Wrath) at the Requiem Mass. Consequently a greater gulf grew between priest and people and between sanctuary and nave. The proceedings at the altar were regarded not so much as something in which to take part, but with wonder and awe. The ceremonial rites which surrounded the Emperor

Constantine at Court were now transferred to the Mass. Hence the use of incense and torches (marks of honor), prostration and bowing, processions and elaborate vestments. The altar rail between priest and people became more elaborate until it finally developed into the "iconostasis," the sanctuary being set aside as a "holy place." Many forms of the Eastern liturgy were developed, each in their own language, and are still in use.

(b) In the West.

While for the Greek period of the Roman Mass we have as guides people like St. Justin, in the West we have very little to go on. Once the language of the Mass had changed from Greek into Latin, it remained in the Latin language alone. Many were the variable texts, according to the season of the church. These gradually took on a fixed form until they developed into our present Roman Canon of the Mass which is quoted by St. Ambrose as far back as the fourth century. The terms themselves "Roman Mass" or "Roman Canon" mean — as done in the City and Diocese of Rome. It is from this time also that we have the three prayers — Collect, Prayer over the Offerings and Post Communion prayer. The Kyrie was substituted for the prayers of intercession, since many of these prayers were contained in the Canon itself. There were processional chants at the beginning, at the Offertory and at the Communion and shorter chants between the lessons. So we see that the framework of the Roman Mass had been determined by the turn of the fifth century.

5. The Papal Mass (6th-7th centuries)

This is so called because Pope Gregory the Great reformed the Roman liturgy. The papacy of those days was a great political as well as spiritual power, and it was easy to have the rights and honors of a king conferred upon the Pope. Ceremonials which really came from the Byzantine-Roman court crept into the Mass — genuflecting, kissing, bowing, and such marks of distinction as incense, candles and the ring. Pope Gregory introduced the Gregorian chant which would accompany the entry, offertory and communion. It was too difficult for the people to sing and was left to the clergy.

6. The Mass of the 8th-11th centuries

In the time of Charlemagne, Church and State almost became one. Charlemagne imposed Catholicism and the Latin liturgy on his entire empire. There was great reverence for the sacrament. About this time, pure white wafers were introduced, as they could be broken easily without the worry of crumbs from the consecrated bread falling to the ground. The offertory procession became more and more rare, and instead of the breaking of bread for the people's communion within the Mass this was done beforehand, or alternatively small hosts such as we have now were provided. Receiving Holy Communion on the tongue instead of in the hand became normal practice, and people received kneeling down. Thus the altar rail was introduced.

It seems that priests and people found the kind of Mass imposed by Charlemagne rather too classical and arid. They began to add their own prayers, such as Psalm 42 and a number of offertory prayers. Genuflections and signs of the cross were added, and the Gospel of St. John at the end of the Mass — and so what began as private devotions slowly became part of the official liturgy.

7. The Mass of the 12th-15th centuries

More and more the role of the people had been reduced to that of spectators. The priest had taken over the roles of reader and chanter, and silent prayers, said by the priest to himself, appeared. Unable to understand or enter into the liturgical meaning of all the priest was doing, the people began to see meaning in his external actions as he moved from one part to another and in the gestures of the Mass. They applied a pious imagination and interpretation to all these things. The five signs of the cross during the canon came to represent the five wounds of Christ; the priest turning around to the people five times during Mass became the five appearances of Christ. The back of the chasuble was embroidered with pictures.

To correct a contemporary heresy denying the real presence of Christ, emphasis was laid upon the Consecration and the bread and wine were elevated. People became obsessed with seeing the host and would rush from church to church as the outdoor bell signalled the Consecration; they would adore the host and then leave. There were prayers to be said while looking upon the host. It was from this that other forms of devotion such as Benediction, processions and expositions of the Blessed Sacrament arose.

There was a multiplication of Guild Chapels and Chantry Chapels (where Mass was "chanted" for the dead). As in early Rome they broke bread in their homes (Acts 2:20), in the early centuries there were domestic Chapels dedicated to the memory of certain martyrs. In later centuries house Chapels were common amongst those who were better off. This practice continued until the Council of Trent. From the house Mass is but a short step to the private Mass. In the monasteries where there were many monks, there would be a series of side altars where each would celebrate, while in the town churches there were guild Chapels for the various guilds. Also there were votive Masses to be said, i.e., Masses for the earnest concerns (vota) of the faithful, and especially for the dead. Since these were not the concern of the whole congregation, they were said privately.

8. The Tridentine Mass of the 16th-20th centuries

The Council of Trent in 1545 set itself to define true Catholic doctrine as against abuse and heresy, and to restore true Christian life within the Church.

For the first time in the history of the Mass, ceremonies were prescribed down to the smallest detail. Rubrics told the priest how he was to keep thumb and finger joined after the Consecration. Everything was to be in complete uniformity throughout the whole church. Pius V published an edition of the breviary and missal to be used in the Roman liturgy, and his successor created the Sacred Congregation of Rites to ensure uniformity throughout. At this point of time they rendered great service in safeguarding the Mass from personal innovations and individual exaggerations. The people, however, unable to take an active part in this great mystery, began to express their own personal devotion in extraliturgical ways such as novenas, devotions to the Sacred Heart, forty hours' devotions. These were in the vernacular and hymns were sung, so they appealed to the people, but they were all outside the structure of the Mass. Indeed, there was an absolute prohibition to translate the Mass books until just before 1900. It is only in our own century that the people have been allowed to read the prayers of the Mass in a missal along with the priest.

9. From Pius X to Vatican II

It was from this time on (1903) that changes began to appear, leading to the major liturgical reforms of the Vatican Council. One of the greatest of these was a decree in 1905 encouraging a return to the practice of the ancient church regarding Communion. Once again Holy Communion was seen as an integral part of the Mass, and people were encouraged to receive Communion weekly, or each time they were at Mass: it is the natural conclusion of the Eucharist. It is from this time also, that children over the age of discretion may receive Communion.

When the people had a text with which to follow the Mass they wanted to recite together the parts which really belonged to them. In 1929 the first uniform text of all the prayers to be read in common was published, although this was very slow to be adopted by the whole church. It led to what became known as the "dialogue Mass." Gradually various parts which had been taken over by the choir went back to the people. Until the Vatican Council, changes were indeed very gradual. In 1955 the ceremonies of Holy Week were restored, and in 1957 permission was given for evening Mass and new regulations for the fast before Communion were introduced.

10. The Mass and Vatican II

As can be seen from what has been described already, Christian worship in the very beginning presupposed full participation by the congregation. The priest led the service, but readers, choir and servers all took their full part in it. The people were involved in the offertory and communion processions, and many of the prayers were in the form of a dialogue between priest and people. But during the Middle Ages the people came to take a less active part.

First of all, they no longer had a command of the language of the liturgy. Then the Introit was no longer an entrance procession but a verse of a psalm recited by the priest at the altar. The readings were no longer intelligible, and indeed were recited by the priest with his back to the people. The offertory contained a great many prayers and no procession. The Canon was prayed in silence. A Gospel reading was added at the very end of the Mass, and additional prayers (the three Hail Marys and other prayers) by Leo XIII. People came along now not so much to take part as "to hear" Mass.

Change can be very upsetting — we hate to lose what we have become familiar with, and change can threaten our security. We hate to see things disappearing which have been hallowed through the ages. But to live is to change, as Cardinal Newman said: "To live is to change, and to be perfect is to have changed often." However, liturgical change must be governed by strict principles; it is not something arbitrary. To quote Cardinal Newman once again, in his *Essay on the Development of Christian Doctrine,* "Principles require a various application according as persons or circumstances vary, and must be thrown into new shapes according to the form of society which they are to influence." We live in a pilgrim Church which is always in need of reformation and renewal.

It is important to understand that the word "aggiornamento," as used by Pope John, means renewal or adaptation and not innovation. It means going back to liturgical principles and being guided solely by them in making any changes. We must distinguish between what is intrinsic in the life of the Church and her liturgy and what are just the accretions of time and really may conceal the important elements. The unchanging aspect of the Church is that she is the permanent presence of Christ among men in faith and worship and life. But in order to remain the same in a changing world, the Church must change too. She is always in history, and not on the immovable shore. From true renewal, the Church should emerge stronger, purer, simpler and more apostolic, and better prepared to announce the Good News to contemporary man. Truth itself doesn't change, but our understanding of it develops, grows and deepens, and reveals itself in different ways. In the Liturgy we have divine mysteries given to us in human form. They inevitably depend on human signs and symbols and words. If those signs are to speak effectively to men, they must evolve and change and adapt as people change.

Pope Paul in opening the fourth Synod of Bishops in 1974 said, "We must be open to what is good and valid in modern experience, without rejecting the past or destroying traditional values. We must not assume that whatever is new must be better, nor that everything traditional must be wrong. Civilisation depends upon tradition. Today we may not be sufficiently aware of the need of stability, for the unchanging and the permanent. The two elements are reconciled within the Godhead, always unchanging and yet ever new, God who is the same yesterday, today and forever."

Even in the time of the Apostles, the Church was faced with the problem of adaptation and renewal. We find it back in the time of St. Paul and the infant Church, in the very first Council of Jerusalem, when he had to fight to liberate the Church from the burden of Jewish Law.

It is interesting to note that the greatest changes of all in the early life of the Church would have been in the liturgy. The early Christian missions were widespread, and in a new area the liturgy was always in the language of the local people. In Rome and the cultural and commercial centers of the Roman Empire it was Greek, but when the Gospel spread out from the cities to the hinterlands of

Egypt, Syria or Armenia the Greek was replaced by the local language. Hence the Greek and Coptic churches all had their own liturgies and languages which we still recognize.

It was about the year 250 that Greek, the original language of the Mass, was replaced by Latin which was now the vernacular. That lasted until the Middle Ages, but since then it has been understood by an ever decreasing number of people. One of the first things that the Vatican Council's Constitution on the Liturgy did was to allow Mass to be in the language of the people once again. It is sometimes said that in a universal church a universal language will bind us all together; but our unity is much deeper than anything that can be achieved through language. It is a spiritual unity in the one Lord and the one Spirit, in the one faith, one baptism, one eucharist, under one leader. In any case, the Mass rite is essentially the same wherever we are; so if we have a missal and we are abroad in a country where we don't understand the language, we can still follow, as we did in the past. A living liturgy requires a living language: the Mass is not only an act of worship, it also has important catechetical and pastoral dimensions.

The Council stated that "active, intelligent and easy participation of all is the purpose of the reforms." New stress was laid on the dignity of the individual Christian as a son of God and this was the basis for all liturgical reforms. "The liturgy is for man, and not man for the liturgy," said Pope Paul, then Cardinal Montini, in one of the early sessions.

Each succeeding cultural epoch had overlaid the original plan of the Mass-liturgy with its own layer and the basic idea itself had been obscured. So in the Constitution on the Liturgy, Vatican II stated: "The rite of the Mass is to be revised in such a way that the intrinsic nature and purpose of its several parts, as also the connection between them, can be more clearly manifested, and so that devout and active participation by the faithful can be more easily accomplished. For this purpose the rites are to be simplified, while due care is taken to preserve their substance. Elements which, with the passage of time, came to be duplicated or were added with little advantage are now to be discarded. When opportunity allows or necessity demands other elements which have suffered injury through accidents of history are now to be restored." (50)

The prayers at the foot of the altar (Psalm 42) which originally the priest was supposed to say on the way from the sacristy to the altar, and which had grown into the Mass, were to be removed. The Introit was to be once again the hymn to accompany the entrance procession. There was to be one act of penance for both priest and people, instead of the priest saying the Confiteor by himself followed by the people saying it and even repeating it again just before Communion. The lessons were once again to be read by the reader, in the vernacular and with both an Old Testament and a New Testament lesson. The prayers of intercession, which were there as far back as the year 150 in the account of the Mass by St. Justin, were to be restored. For the liturgy of the Eucharist the priest was to face the people as he did in the early church, so that they could see and respond. Once again there was to be a real Offertory procession and hymn; and, instead of five long offertory prayers, two simple prayers inspired by those Christ would have said at the Jewish Passover meal. There were to be three additional Eucharistic prayers, all of them drawing heavily upon similar prayers in the very early church.

The whole rite was to be simpler, with fewer genuflections, fewer signs of the cross, and kissing the altar only at the beginning and end. The ancient custom of acclaiming the Risen Christ after the Consecration was to be revived, as was the kiss of peace. The dismissal was to come in its rightful place at the very end of the Mass instead of before the blessing. The Gospel of St. John was removed from the end of the Mass, since it was originally part of the priest's private thanksgiving and had grown into the Mass, and was rather incongruous outside the liturgy of the Word. The prayers which followed (three Hail Marys, Hail Holy Queen) had all been added successively by Leo XIII, Pius IX and Pius X and were dropped, since the Mass had ended with the dismissal, and the appropriate place to pray for any special intention was during the prayers of intercession. Four years after the Council, all these recommendations were implemented by the Apostolic Constitution, *Missale Romanum,* (April 1969) which set the form of the Mass that we now have.

Just as the early Christian rite was simple, unadorned and confined to essentials — so this new rite of the Mass has a noble simplicity that lifts us up to God. Each person or group — priest, readers, choir, servers and congregation — must do their part well, conscious of what they are about. They must invest it with a sense of the numinous or holy. The principal Sunday Mass is made more solemn with incense, acolytes and a Gospel and Offertory procession. So, through true renewal, the texts and rites of the Mass express ever more clearly the holy things they signify.

3

The Mass Explained

Opening Rites of the Mass

Entrance procession and hymn

When possible, the priest and the servers should make their entrance from the back of the Church, so that it is a real procession, and this should be accompanied by a hymn or chant. Singing in this way expresses our joy as we gather together for worship in God's house. It also helps to unite us as a community, as we join together in singing God's praises. The hymn should be chosen as one suitable for the beginning of worship, and appropriate for the season or feast. In Advent it will express our longing for Christ; at Easter, our joy in the risen Lord. If there is no entrance song, the entrance antiphon is recited.

Kissing the Altar

It is the salutation of the place where the mystery of the Eucharist is to be celebrated. In pre-Christian times, it was often the practice to honor the Temple by kissing the threshold. This custom was continued in christendom by kissing the altar around which the faithful gather for the Supper of the Lord. It is to be found in the liturgy as early as the fourth century.

Incensing the Altar

It is highly desirable on the occasion of important feasts, and at the principal Sunday Mass, that incense should be used. It has been used in worship from the very earliest times. In Judaism it was a mark of honor and a symbol of our prayers rising up to God, "Let my prayer come before you like incense." (Psalm 141:v.2). Thus, it was always present on the altar during Old Testament worship (Lev. 16:12).

I think it is extremely important in these days when some people feel that the Mass lacks a sense of the numinous, or the sacred, that we keep such ancient symbols as these in order to give it a certain solemnity.

We still use it as a mark of honor, and thus we incense the altar, the Gospel book, the bread and wine, the Crucifix, the priest and the people. It can be for us also a sign of our thoughts and prayers rising up to God.

Sign of the Cross

The priest and the people begin the Mass by making the Sign of the Cross together. This is done to remind us of Christ who died on the Cross, and to recall the triune God: Father, Son and Holy Spirit, by whose power we begin and end all things. He is the Alpha and Omega. We sign ourselves to show that we are God's people. It was at Baptism that the priest first traced this sign on our foreheads: the sign of the Christian.

The Greeting

When we meet one another in everyday life, we usually begin with some form of greeting. In our revised Mass we have three forms of greeting, all taken from the Scriptures. The first two are from St. Paul, "The Grace of Our Lord Jesus Christ and the love of God and the fellowship of the Holy Spirit be with you all," (2 Cor: 13. 14), or "The grace and peace of God our Father and the Lord Jesus Christ be with you." (Eph: 6. 23). It is probable that these two formulas were used at the early Christian Mass, since St. Paul's epistles would be read out to the assembled community and following the conclusion of his letter (which ended with the above phrases) the Eucharist would then be celebrated.

The third greeting, "The Lord be with you," has long been familiar to us. It goes right back to the Old Testament days. When Boaz went out to greet Ruth and the reapers in the cornfield, he did so with the words: "The Lord be with you," and they returned the greeting with the words, "The Lord bless you." The angel Gabriel greeted Our Lady in a similar way. It is a delightful greeting, reminding us that God is here present among his assembled people: the people reciprocate by saying, "And also with you," asking that God may be present too with the priest in the exercise of his ministry.

This special greeting is repeated at important moments during the Mass, for example: to introduce the Gospel, in the dialogue before the Preface and before dismissal at the end of the Mass.

Introducing the Mass

At this point, the priest has the opportunity of giving a brief introduction to the Mass of the day. This should do no more than indicate the feast or major theme of the Mass being celebrated and invite the people to open and dispose their hearts to receiving this message.

The Act of Penance

Our Lord has told us that before offering our gift at the altar we must first be reconciled with our brother. (Matthew 5: 24). A gift is only of value in life insofar as it represents the giver. Sin is not just our own private affair — it offends against God and our neighbor. We are less worthy members of the whole Christian community because of our sinfulness, hence the need to say we are sorry to God and to one another. God's forgiveness restores a wholeness to our lives which then makes us more worthy to make our own offering. (It is interesting how our word, "scape-goat," comes from the Old Testament Jewish custom of symbolically unloading their sins upon a goat which they then drove out into the wilderness. Thus cleansed, they would then offer sacrifice.)

After making our confession to God in silence, we have a choice of three forms of Penance. The first is a revised version of the "Confiteor," which, in its previous form, had been part of the Mass since 1570. The second consists of two short phrases asking for forgiveness. In the third act of Penance ending, "Lord have mercy," the priest may substitute his own phrases for those given in the missal. The Asperges may also be used here introducing the baptismal symbol of water.

God's Forgiveness

The Absolution then follows. This is a true forgiveness of all venial sins, since we have expressed our sorrow in the above prayers.

Lord have mercy

This is familiar under the old Greek name "Kyrie" which means "Lord." It came into our church from the Eastern Liturgy. One of the deacons would read a list of petitions and as he spoke each of the names, a crowd of boys who stood there answered him each time "Kyrie eleison." In other words, it was the response to the prayers of the faithful, or a litany which in the early centuries was placed at the first part of the Mass.

In the sixth century, Pope St. Gregory the Great found certain liturgical celebrations rather long, and so decided to omit the "prayers of the faithful" but retained the triple response, "Lord have mercy," in honor of the three persons of the Trinity. This remains unaltered in its present position, even though the "prayers of the faithful" have now been restored just before the offertory procession.

Glory to God in the Highest

This comes from a collection of Church hymns which were written for divine service in the early Church. It is divided into three parts: — (1) The song of the angels on the night of the Nativity as recorded by Luke 2: 14; (2) The praise of God as we address him by his various titles; (3) The invoking of Christ.

It was intended as a festival song and was introduced into the Mass during the fifth century, first of all to be sung at the Christmas Mass. By the eleventh century it was being sung on all Sundays and important feasts during the year. This is why we still omit it at times of penance such as Advent and Lent — so as not to anticipate the joy of the feast itself.

Collect

While the priest says the Collect, he stands with hands upraised. This raising of the arms heavenwards is a fitting accompaniment to the prayer that rises to him who dwells in heaven (You will notice that the priest does this many times during the Mass — prayer over the offerings, preface, Canon, Our Father and the Post-communion prayer). All these prayers have been his since the early days of the church and he says them on behalf of the whole congregation as the one who presides. Everybody stands during these prayers. This was the normal posture for prayer among ancient peoples, as a means of honoring a higher being. It was only very gradually that kneeling came in for certain parts of the Mass, and was only general from the thirteenth century. It developed from the bowing of the head which had been customary for certain prayers.

In this prayer the priest "collects" the spiritual needs of the community and presents them to the Father, through the Son, in the Holy Spirit.

Amen

How many times we say this word! So short and yet so rich in meaning. It is a Hebrew word and since it is hard to find the exact equivalent in the vernacular, it has been adopted without translation into each and every form of liturgy. If one attempted to convey its meaning, the equivalent word would be something like "so be it." It is our "yes" or assent, confirming the prayer that has just been offered. We must say it with great firmness and assurance.

Liturgy of the Word

The word "liturgy" comes from a Greek word meaning the form of service or regular ritual of the church. At this part of the Mass, the service is centered around the "Word" — God's Word which we find in the Scripture. The Vatican Council document on the liturgy said: "The treasures of the Bible are to be opened up more lavishly, so that a richer fare may be provided for the faithful at the Table of God's Word. Therefore a more representative portion of the Holy Scriptures will be read to the people over a set cycle of years."

Old Testament Reading

People must sometimes wonder if it was necessary to restore an Old Testament reading to the Mass, and what relevance it could possibly have to our lives. To understand this we must bear in mind three things: (1) It is God speaking to us no less in the Old Testament than in the New Testament; all Scripture is inspired by God; whatever was written in former days was written for our instruction. "We were to derive hope from that message of endurance and courage which the Scriptures bring us." (Rom. 15: 4). Therefore it is very important to keep in mind that it *is* God himself who is addressing us. Through the people and events of the Old Testament he reveals himself to us (for instance his love and faithfulness) and our responsibility to him (as shown in the Ten Commandments or the messages of his prophets).

(2) The people portrayed in the Bible are real people with the same kind of human problems and difficulties we experience today. In speaking to and through them, God

51

was speaking to us. God had created the world and placed man above all creatures; Adam's sin changed God's plan toward man, but not his love. After man's rejection, God made a second call, this time through Abraham who accepted and showed great faith. In Abraham, God selected and blessed above all others a single people, Israel. With the deliverance of the Israelites from the bondage of the Egyptians, a nation, God's chosen people, was born. God gave Moses the leadership and through him, the Ten Commandments. Thereafter, through leaders, Judges, Kings and prophets, God directed and guided his people and eventually brought them to the promised land.

In spite of God's love the majority remained unfaithful, often turning completely from God to the worship of idols. In comparison to the nation as a whole, those who remained faithful were few. The returned exiles from Babylon were but a remnant of the race, but they became the heart and core of approved Jewish belief. According to God's plan these selected few laid the foundation of the Holy Land which later became the scene of the Redeemer's life on earth. God's coming was drawing near — Christ came to live among men — the Old Testament ended and the New Testament began.

(3) The events of the past have their meaning for us today. We now are the new Israelites, in exile on earth but on our journey to the promised land, our heavenly home. We also are tempted and rebellious and yet God remains faithful and forgiving. People like Abraham are still an example to us of faith, prophets such as Isaiah still call on us to straighten out the way and prepare a place for God in our hearts. Job is still an example to us of how to bear suffering. Symbols such as water, giving life in the desert, foreshadowed the life-giving waters of Baptism. God fed his chosen people with manna during their pilgrim journey, and now he feeds us on the Eucharist.

And so, through people and events of the Old Testament God still speaks to us today. He reveals himself to us; we see his dealings with people and can identify with them and thus learn of our responsibility to him. In these stories of his dealings with men we learn of his underlying care and concern for the welfare of man, and also that these happenings are not just history or merely past events. It reminds us that God is still concerned, still loves, still cares.

Responsorial Psalm

This is so called because the people having listened to God's Word, now respond to his message. Frequently the response echoes the theme of the first reading; it is very concise and usually sums up the mood of the psalm. I spoke about the psalms in the first chapter and said how they were cries of joy, sorrow, despair and praise.

New Testament reading

The Old Testament reading prepares the way for the New, in which it finds it fulfilment. There is always a link between one of these readings and the Gospel. In Lent and Advent it will be the Old Testament reading which is more in keeping with the Gospel, as it points to the main stages in God's preparation of his people for the gift of salvation. There is three year cycle of Sunday readings and, with exceptions, there is one main theme which pre-dominates at each Mass. The main theme is usually to be found in the Old Testament reading and the Gospel.

The second reading is more concerned with Christian living and it is often a continuous passage read over the course of a number of weeks, which means that its message will not always be the same as that of the other readings. It is very important that the Word of God evokes a response within us. If we believe that it is really God's Word then we must ask ourselves what message he is addressing to us and judge our lives by our confrontation with the Word. Sometimes there may be a moment of silence after the reading, so that we may do this.

We acknowledge that God himself speaks to us as the reader ends the lesson by saying, "This is the Word of the Lord." Our response is, "Thanks be to God," who has spoken to us through his Word.

The Alleluia Verse

This is a word of greeting and welcome to Christ who is to speak to us through the words of the Gospel. Like the "Amen," it is impossible to translate and so remained in Hebrew. It originated as a sign of welcome at the Easter Mass and then found its way into the Sunday liturgy, since, as I said in the first chapter, every Sunday is a "little Easter." Being a compound of two Hebrew words meaning "Praise God," and because it expresses triumphant praise, it is better sung. It is followed by a short phrase taken usually from one of the readings or the Gospel which is to follow, thereby echoing its message.

Gospel

This last of the three readings holds the highest rank, since it is always about Christ — what he has said or done. The word "Gospel" means "Good news," since the tidings of Christ are full of promise, hope and victory. We can see what care people bestowed on the Gospels by the number of illuminated manuscripts and miniatures that decorate the books of the Gospels. The Lindisfarne Gospels now in the British museum are famous among the first and most splendid of illustrated manuscripts in Western Europe. They belong to the 7th century, being earlier and more elaborate than the Book of Kells done in Ireland in the 9th century. Both books portray the Icon of Christ; we also are meant to be the Icon or image of Christ by living the Gospel.

The Gospel book is shown the same honor as a person, since Christ comes among us in the form of his Word; "It is he himself who speaks whenever the Scriptures are read in church." (Sc. 7). The book may be carried in during the entrance procession and placed upon the altar as a sign of Christ coming among his people. At the time of the Gospel reading it is again carried in procession and may be accompanied by incense and acolytes — marks of honor as shown to a person. The people stand for this reading and sign their foreheads, lips and hearts to show that they believe, speak and live by the Word of Christ. The Gospel may be proclaimed only by the priest (or deacon) and on special occasions in the early church, it was reserved to the Bishop and would be proclaimed from the rood loft — the highest point. At the end of the Gospel reading, the priest kisses the book and once again the people address Christ directly as a person. They say, "Praise to you, Lord Jesus Christ."

Homily

In the fourth chapter of St. Luke we read, "Jesus went into the synagogue on the Sabbath day as he usually did. He stood up to read and they handed him the scroll of the prophet Isaiah — then he began to speak to them." Thus the synagogue service took the form of a reading followed by a commentary, and our Mass does the same. The function of the homily is to break the bread of God's Word for the people. The Word is not just a record of past events, but is meant to have an immediate bearing on our lives; it summons us to a present decision. The homily has to make clear this present relevance of the Word. To do this the homily must first explain the meaning of the message and give the people a true understanding of it. In this respect the priest endeavors to do what Christ did on the road to Emmaus, ". . . he interpreted to them in all the Scriptures, the things concerning himself." (Lk. 24: 27).

Secondly, the link must be shown between the message and the actual life of the people in all its present reality. Thus will emerge the force of God's Word as a present invitation and summons, saving those who accept, judging those who refuse.

So, the homily develops some point from the readings of the Mass of the day, explaining its timeless message and applying it to the needs of the particular community.

Creed

Having listened to the Word in the readings and homily, we now stand and profess our faith in what God has revealed to us. The Nicene Creed, composed at the Council of Nicea in 325 A.D., became an ancient Baptismal formula recited by those about to be received into the church. This is why it began in the singular "I believe," which has now been changed to "We believe," since it is appropriate that the profession of faith made by the Christian people gathered for the Eucharist should be in the plural.

The Creed is a resumé of salvation history, divided basically into three parts, expressing our belief in God the Father — creator; God the Son who died and rose again; and God the Holy Spirit. Much of it was inspired by Eph. 4: 4. which emphasizes the importance of unity: "One Lord, one faith, one baptism." Hence the "oneness" of God is stressed and the "oneness" of His revelation against all division; "We believe in one God, one Lord, one catholic and apostolic church . . . we acknowledge one baptism. . . ."

Prayer of the Faithful

As early as 150 A.D., St. Justin tells us at this part of the Mass, "We all stand up and recite prayers." In the early Church the petitions were offered in nine parts as in the Good Friday liturgy today. During the late Middle Ages this fell into disuse, although in some countries it persisted under the form of one prayer embracing all the intentions. Now, it has been restored, and we relate our prayer life to our daily needs as we pray for the Church, the World and our local communities. First of all, it should be inspired by the theme of the day and secondly, express concern for the needs of people in both the secular and religious areas of life. It should relate to the present and arise from our present day needs, otherwise it will seem irrelevant and somewhat dead. These prayers should be expressed in the form of commendations; they are addressed to the people rather than direct prayers to God.

We then pray to Our Lady. There follows a period of silence during which we commend our intentions to God and the priest then concludes with a final prayer.

Liturgy of the Eucharist

This comprises three parts.
(1) Preparation of the gifts.
(2) Eucharist Prayer.
(3) Communion rite.

Preparation of the Gifts: Bread

There can be little doubt that the bread used by Christ at the Last Supper was the unleavened bread prescribed for the Paschal meal — bread made of fine wheat flour. Occasionally leavened bread (the ordinary domestic bread) was allowed, making it easier for people to bring their own. Since the eleventh century however, the use of leavened bread in the Western rites is prohibited because of a concern to make the Eucharistic bread more distinctive. In ancient times there was a practice of stamping the bread with a symbol or inscription. Today, it is usually a cross or the Alpha and Omega — first and last letters of the Greek alphabet. The Mass bread is known as a host, from the Latin "hostia," meaning a sacrificial lamb.

Today, we are encouraged to use thicker hosts which look more genuinely like food and which may be broken and given to a small number present. This expresses more clearly the unity of sharing in the same meal.

Wine

With regard to the second element — the wine — white or red wine can be used as long as it is, "natural wine from the fruit of the vine, pure and unmixed with any foreign substance." (GI 284*) This is because of the belief that Christ used pure grape wine as indicated by St. Luke 22:18. "I shall not drink of the fruit of the vine again, till the Kingdom of God has come."

The Psalmist tells us how wine stands for joy and he praises God who enables us to ". . . bring forth bread from the earth and wine to cheer man's heart." (Ps 103:25). The priest adds a little water to the wine thus symbolizing

*GI — General Instruction on the Roman Missal.

the intimate union of the faithful with him. This is expressed in the prayer which accompanies it, "By the mystery of this water and wine may we come to share in the divinity of Christ who humbled himself to share in our humanity." This practice of diluting wine with water was current in our Lord's time, and necessary because of the viscous quality of the wine. The Church very quickly gave it a religious significance and it became a sign of the coming together of the human and the divine. In the same way as the wine receives the water in itself, so has Christ taken to himself us and our sins.

Money collection

Because all gifts come from God and we should use them to the glory of his name, from the very earliest times the action in which the Lord's body and blood are offered up began to include the presentation of material gifts which are drawn into the liturgical celebration. By the time we reach St. Cyprian (early third century), it had become a general rule that the faithful should present gifts at the Sunday Mass. In fact, we find an instance of Cyprian admonishing a rich woman for her lack of charity in failing to bring a gift!

One had to make an offering to the community poor box as well as bringing some bread and wine. It had become customary to think of every gift to the church and the poor as a gift to God and so the two blend together. Whatever was left over from material gifts, as well as bread and wine, was given to the poor. Later centuries had the tithe barns, built near the church to house one tenth of the produce of land or stock which would have been donated by each person.

For a long time these gifts have been in the form of money, some of which will still be given away to various charitable purposes. It is very desirable that this should form a part of the offertory procession and as the priest receives the collection he could offer it up in these or similar words, "Lord, everything in heaven and on earth is yours, all things come from you, and of your own do we give you." (1 Chronicles 29:16).

Procession

In the new rite, we are encouraged, certainly at the principal Sunday Mass, to have an offertory procession carrying the bread and wine and collection of money taken from the people at this point.

As we have just seen, this was current practice in the early church, but by the tenth century the custom had fallen into disuse, partly because of the change from material goods to money, and partly because the necessary income of the church of those days was assured for the most part by fixed possessions and by prescribed taxes. The Church however still retained an offertory procession on certain feast days, but by the seventeenth century this too had fallen into disuse.

The bringing up of the gifts is important to the new rite. It must be done well and with reverence. Often a server will lead them. This procession of lay people through the church and up to the altar underlines strongly the people's part in the Mass.

Offertory chant

Just as the entrance of the clergy at the beginning of the Mass was accompanied by a chant, so too, is the offertory procession enriched by an appropriate chant expressing joy as the people offer their gifts, for, "God loves a cheerful giver." This song may reflect something about our act of offering and about the season we are in, or may be a general hymn. Its main purpose is to bind us together in what we are doing and to accompany the procession. From time to time the offertory song can be replaced with quiet organ music, or with silence.

The prayers

The two prayers which accompany the offering of the bread and wine are very beautiful and are modelled on Jewish blessing prayers and they praise God who gives us everything that we have: "Blessed are you, Lord, God of all creation. Through your goodness we have this bread to offer, which earth has given and human hands have made. It will become for us the bread of life."

The Jewish form, recited by our Lord whenever he blessed bread at the beginning of a meal and still in use by pious Jews today is; "Blessed are you, Lord our God, King of the world, who caused bread to come forth from the earth," (over the wine . . . "who gave us this fruit of the vine").

Incensation

It is interesting to learn that in Roman usage incense was carried only at the entrance procession, the procession of the Gospel book and at the procession at the end of Mass. There was no real incensation — this came in the ninth century in Carolingian times and greater prominence was given to the incensation at this part of the Mass, since it included not only the gifts, but also the altar, crucifix and people. Thus things and people are hallowed and enveloped in an atmosphere of prayer and dedication.

It is an expressive sign as the incense which is consumed in the charcoal rises heavenwards in fragrant clouds to God, so that in turn his benediction may descend upon us.

The washing of hands

It is natural when we take part in something holy that we approach it with reverence and prepare for it in certain ways. Thus the priest puts on special vestments and washes his hands.

The people also must be cleansed and so at the entrance of the ancient Christian basilica was a fountain or well used for this purpose. In the same way Muslims wash their hands and feet before entering a Mosque. This is the origin of the holy water stoop now in our churches from which we bless ourselves as we enter. It was also customary to sprinkle the people with holy water (Asperges) at the beginning of the principal Sunday Mass. Both of these actions are a form of cleansing rite and recall the waters of baptism. So the washing of the hands by the priest means he must be inwardly cleansed (he recites a verse from Psalm 50, "Lord, wash away my iniquity, cleanse me from my sins") before commencing the solemn Eucharistic prayer.

"Pray brethren;" . . . now that the arrangement of all the gifts has been completed and the priest is about the begin the Last Supper prayer of Christ, he stretches out his arms and call upon all present to join him in prayer. This prayer has a rather personal character and is to be found very early on in the history of the Mass.

Prayer over the Offerings

This is the second of the three great priestly prayers. Just as the entrance rite concludes with the Collect and the Communion with the Post-communion prayer, so the oblation concludes with the prayer recited over the gifts. Like the other two prayers, it varies according to the church year, but is always the same in structure and design. It is in the plural and usually expresses the idea that we have come to offer these gifts to God, may he sanctify them and so transformed may they be a help for our lives.

This concludes the presentation of the gifts and heralds the Eucharist prayer which is about to begin.

Eucharistic Prayer

We come now to what the Vatican Council describes as the "centre and climax of the whole celebration." (GI 54). It begins with the dialogue before the Preface and ends when the priest holds up both the host and the chalice together and says: "through him, with him, in him. . . ."

We have four Eucharistic prayers with the words of institution more or less the same in all four — only the narratives in which they are set are different. The purpose of this prayer is to praise and thank God for all he has done for us, which is what the Greek word "Eucharist" means. It is a Christianised form of a Jewish prayer used by our Lord at the Last Supper.

The first Eucharistic prayer, the "Roman" Canon as it is known, has been used since the fourth century. To provide variety and to add richness to our expression of praise and thanksgiving at this part, we now thave three other Eucharistic prayers, all of them old in origin. Eucharistic prayer II, as it is called, is very short, simple and clear. It was written by a Roman priest called Hippolytus in the third century. The third Eucharistic prayer is based on the Alexandrian Eucharistic prayer of St. Basil and goes back to the fourth century. The last Eucharistic prayer is a longer one and recalls the history of our salvation. It would seem very appropriate for occasional use in Advent and Lent, and for special groups. It is theologically very rich and, although a new composition, is based on traditional material from oriental prayers.

Dialogue before the Preface

Whereas other prayers of the priest in the Mass are just preceded by, "Let us pray," the Great Prayer of the Canon has a longer and very old exchange between priest and people. This part goes back almost to apostolic times and remains unchanged in the liturgies of both East and West. It begins with the usual greeting, "The Lord be with you," and is followed by, "LIFT UP YOUR HEARTS."

As the priest says this, he opens his hands and raises them up, as a sign of our hearts and minds being lifted up to God. As St. Paul reminds us, "Risen then with Christ, you must lift your thoughts above . . ." (Col. 3:1). We must rise above all earthly things, and at this important part give our minds and hearts solely to God.

The people reply, "We lift them up to the Lord." Let us mean what we say, so that God does not reproach us as he did the people of the Old Testament, "These people worship me with their lips, but their hearts are far from me." In the Greek liturgies the sacrificial prayer is known as the Anaphora, which means "the lifting up." Let us be lifted up in heart and mind as we approach the Great Prayer of the Mass.

In the last part of this dialogue the priest invites the people, "LET US GIVE THANKS TO THE LORD OUR GOD." The Eucharistic prayer, as we shall see, is all about thanksgiving. In order to introduce this theme, the priest now invites us to give thanks to God and the people show their willingness to do this, "It is right to give him thanks and praise." And so, having lifted up our hearts, we now prepare to thank God in the part that follows.

Preface

This prayer is a proclamation of the adoration, praise and thanksgiving that we owe to God. All this will be proclaimed in a different way by a rich variety of eighty prefaces in the new Roman missal for the various seasons, Sundays and feasts. With joy we join our praises with the heavenly choirs in adoring God.

The Sanctus

This is a continuation of the preface, but since it reminds us that the 'earthly church,' should take part in the heavenly singing, all the people join together in reciting or singing this part. Few texts have inspired such beautiful musical setting as the Sanctus. We have only to think, for example, of Fauré's requiem. The words come from the prophet Isaiah, who had a vision of seraphs praising God, "And they cried out to one another in this way, 'Holy, holy, holy is Yahweh Sabaoth. His glory fills the whole earth.' " (Isaiah 6:3). The title 'Sabaoth' comes from the Hebrew and means 'Lord of Hosts.'

The phrase, "Heaven and earth are full of your glory," was added in Christian liturgies to emphasize that it was no longer the Temple of Jerusalem that echoed with the triple Sanctus but that the focus had now been switched to heaven. "Blessed is he who comes. . . ." This is from psalm 118 and means that it is from heaven that Christ will come to save us. Hosanna! A Hebrew word of acclaim to God.

The bell used to be rung at this point to signal the approach of the Consecration, and to express joy. In medieval times the practice arose of ringing an outdoor bell at the *Ter Sanctus* so that those unable to attend might pause and pray, and so associate themselves with the service. In many old churches Sanctus bell turrets or apertures in the West wall still exist, giving a view of the altar from the ringing chamber.

First Invocation

The priest now begins one of the four Eucharist prayers. They begin with praise and thanks, and then invoke the Holy Spirit to come down and hallow these gifts, "So that they may become the body and blood of our Lord Jesus Christ." The priest places his hands over the gifts as a sign of invoking the Holy Spirit.

Narrative of Institution

St. Matthew describes the Last Supper in these words, "Jesus took bread, and blessed, and broke it and gave it to his disciples saying, 'Take, eat, this is my body.' " (Matt. 26:26).

In order really to understand what is happening here, we need to understand what would happen at a normal Jewish Paschal supper. We tend to think of the Last Supper just as a meal; in fact it was an act of worship in meal form, instituted by Moses at God's command to commemorate the liberation of the Jews from the slavery of Egypt. Every devout Jew would observe this, either at home or with friends. It followed a very strict ritual over which the head of the family presided and said the main prayer of praise and thanksgiving. He took bread and blessed it, said the grace over it, giving thanks to God, and broke it. He would then do the same with the cup of wine at the end of the meal. "When supper was ended. . . ." Both were given to all present.

It was this very action that Christ was going to use to perpetuate his sacrifice on Calvary. He took bread in the normal way, and having blessed it and given thanks, he broke it and added, "This is my body which will be given up for you." In the same way he took the cup and also thanked God, but then added, "This is the cup of my blood, the blood of the new and everlasting Covenant. It will be shed for you and for all men, so that sins may be forgiven."

And so, in the Mass, the meal aspect has not changed, nor has the theme of thanksgiving. What is different is the memorial aspect of the meal. Instead of recalling the wonders God did for the people of the Old Testament in freeing them from slavery in Egypt, and the Covenant (testament) sealed in their own blood of the circumcision, we now do it in memory of me, (that is, Christ) who by his death has brought us, the new chosen people, out of the slavery of sin through his blood on the cross. This is the new and everlasting Covenant as opposed to the old Covenant.

It is a wonderful moment, when there is a real identification of Christ and the priest. In the person of the priest Christ himself stands at the altar, takes the bread and is active in so far as it is by virtue of power deriving from him that the bread and wine become his body and blood. The risen Christ is now present in our midst. We have the elevation of the bread and wine and at the same time we have the ringing of the bell to direct attention to what is happening.

Proclamation of the Mystery of Faith

In oriental liturgies, after the words of Consecration comes an ancient profession of faith in Greek, "We believe and confess and profess." In the Roman Mass, by the end of the Middle Ages a solemn salutation of the Blessed Sacrament at the elevation formed part of the ceremony at High Mass. Hymns were sung in honor of the Blessed Sacrament, but this custom did not last long. In our present Mass we are invited once again to join in acclaiming Christ after the Consecration. Although the Eucharistic prayer is of its nature uniquely the prayer of the priest, as the one who presides over the community (as it was the prayer of the head of the Jewish family as he presided at the meal) and he is the one who in the name of the people voices thanksgiving, the people associate themselves with this prayer on four occasions: First of all in the preface dialogue, which begins the Eucharistic prayer; then in praising God in the Sanctus; then they join in acclaiming Christ, and they conclude the Canon with the Great Amen. The four acclamations: "Christ has died," and the others are more than just a salutation, they express our faith in the passion, death and resurrection of Christ and that he will come again in glory at the end of time.

The Memorial Prayer

"Do this in memory of me," comes as Christ's command to do what he had done — an injunction to repeat his action. It means a recalling and actualizing of past events. Hence the prayer after the Consecration expresses this idea, "In memory of his death and resurrection, we offer you, Father, this life-giving bread." (Eucharistic prayer II) "Father, calling to mind the death your son endured for our salvation. . . . we offer you in thanksgiving this holy and living sacrifice." (Eucharistic prayer III).

Second Invocation

The type of invocation varies according to the Eucharistic prayer. In the first prayer we ask God to, "Look with favor on these offerings," and to accept them as He did those of the Old Testament. The other three Eucharistic prayers invoke the unifying power of the Holy Spirit, "And by your Holy Spirit, gather all who share this one bread and one cup into the one body of Christ." (Eucharistic prayer IV).

The Intercessions

At this moment we celebrate the Eucharist in union with the whole church, both in heaven and on earth, and we offer it for all members both living and dead, as we share in the redemption of Christ. Therefore these intercessions fall mainly into three groups:

a. For the church — bishops, clergy and people and "all who seek you with a sincere heart."

b. For the dead, "whose faith is known to you alone."

c. In communion with all the saints: we call upon the help of all those who have witnessed to Christ through the ages.

The Great Amen

This follows on the priest's conclusion, "Through him, with him. . . ." as he holds up the gifts, not just for the people to see but as an oblation to God. On many occasions we say "Amen" in the Mass, but this is known as "the Great Amen" since it is the whole affirmation of the people to what has been done in the Eucharistic action. They join in the thanksgiving and offering of Christ. If this is so, it is sad that many congregations make such a half-hearted response! St. Jerome tells us how the Great Amen used to resound like a thunderclap all around the basilica. St. Augustine calls it our signature to the Mass. St. Justin, as we have seen, in his early account of the Mass tells "How the whole crowd standing cries out in agreement, 'Amen!' " Just as we began the Eucharistic prayer with an important dialogue to the preface, we now end this prayer with a long and impressive conclusion which should be said by the priest alone. At sung Masses the people may then come in with a triple "Amen!" But whether sung or said, may this Amen be a really heartfelt conclusion, associating ourselves in as full a way as possible with this great act of thanksgiving.

Communion

"Let us pray our confidence to the Father. . . ."
When we think of God as our Father it should inspire us with confidence, and so we recall this fact before we ask God for our daily needs in the Lord's prayer. This introduction by the priest may be varied.

The Our Father

The Communion rite really begins with the Lord's prayer. Two petitions in the prayer make this particularly appropriate. "Give us this day our daily bread, and forgive us our trespasses as we forgive. . . ." In the first place we ask for the bread of life, which in this context means the body of Christ, although we may have in mind our needs for each day. In the second petition we pray for reconciliation with God and with our neighbor before Communion.

This prayer has certainly been part of the Mass since the fourth century and probably very much earlier. The last phrase: "deliver us from evil. . . ." is then developed in the prayer that follows. In response to it there is an acclamation: "For the kingdom, the power and the glory are yours, now and forever." This comes at the end of the Our Father because the Jews had a practice of ending each prayer with a prayer of praise. Although it has been newly restored to the Mass, one can trace its origin as far back as the second century, and it is given with the Our Father in some manuscripts of St. Matthews's Gospel.

The Rite of Peace

Holy Communion is above all the sacrament of unity. It signifies union with God and with one another. This unity is broken by sin and disharmony and so we now pray that we may be at peace with God and with one another, "Lord Jesus Christ, you said to your apostles, 'I leave you peace. . . .'" The risen Christ always greeted his disciples with the words, "Peace be with you," and so this greeting of Christ is now given to the people. The accompanying sign or kiss of peace is very old indeed. We read about it in the account of the Mass by St. Justin in the year 150 A.D., "After finishing the prayers, we greet each other with a holy kiss." It has taken many forms down the centuries. At one time the "pax," as it was known, was a representation of the Lord's passion, and was kissed by the priest at the words, "The peace of the Lord be with you always," and afterwards passed around to be kissed by the congregation. Finally the rite was reduced to the kissing of the altar, and the kiss of peace given by the clergy to one another at a High Mass. Now it has been restored, and should convey a deeply felt sign of friendship, peace and reconciliation with one another.

The Breaking of Bread

We recall that this is what Jesus did at the Last Supper, "He took bread, said the blessing, broke the bread. . . ." This was so significant that in early times the Mass was known as "the Breaking of Bread." The significance lies in the fact that, in sharing the one bread, we show our unity with one another. In the early days when they broke bread at the Pope's Mass, the Deacon then took Holy Communion to the other churches in Rome. As St. Paul said, "The one bread makes us one body, and though we are many in number the same bread is shared by all." (1 Cor. 10:17). A small portion of the host is put into the chalice containing the precious Blood to emphasize the oneness of the Body and Blood of Christ. Since the breaking of bread could take a very long time, certain hymns were sung. Today only one remains, the "Lamb of God," where we invoke Christ's power to save us.

Prayer before Communion

The priest now bows down and has a choice of two prayers which he says silently. The people may also use this moment for a brief period of silent prayer before Communion.

Holy Communion

The priest now shows the host to the people and calls upon the Lamb of God to take away our sins. (John 1:36). A delightful phrase has now been added to this, taken from the book of the Apocalypse, "Happy are those who are called to his supper." And then the well known words of the centurion, "Lord, I am not worthy. . . ." (Matt. 8:9). The Communion is given to the people, accompanied by

72

the words, "The body of Christ . . . the blood of Christ." These formulas are both very old, and can be found as far back as the third century. The people answer, "Amen." St. Ambrose, writing in the fourth century, warned the people, "Not idly therefore do you say "Amen," for you are confessing that you receive the body of Christ. When, then, you present yourself the priest says, "The body of Christ" and you answer "Amen," that is, it is true. What you confess with your lips, keep in your heart."

After Communion

The priest cleanses the sacred vessels either now or after the Mass is over. The General Instruction on the Mass tells us, "Priest and people may pray in their hearts for some time. A hymn or some other canticle of praise may be sung (or said) by all." When there is period of silence for private prayer, it would seem to me that if the atmosphere is quiet and recollected, this really ought to last for a few minutes rather than for just a few seconds. People complain that there isn't enough silence in the Mass or a time for private prayer. Also, it all ends very soon after Communion is over. This pause provides such an opportunity. We may like to ponder on the theme of the readings or homily, or talk to God about the week that has ended or that which is beginning, or about anything that touches closely upon our lives. Silence is rare these days, and we should value these moments of peace and reflection.

Postcommunion Prayer

The priest now prays that what we have celebrated and received may have its effect in our lives.

Announcements

The Mass is now over effectively. The liturgy of the Eucharist ends with the postcommunion prayer. The announcements come just before the dismissal, since, if they came at any other part, they would break up the sequence of the Mass. They should be brief and serve just to call attention to events that are probably already mentioned in the parish newsletter.

The Blessing

The priest greets the people, and then raises his hands and calls down God's help and protection upon the people as they leave. The people bow before God to receive his blessing. The word "blessing" as used in Scripture has many meanings: praise, divine favor, prayer that God shall be with a certain person or thing, dedication of a person or thing to a sacred purpose. In the Old Testament a blessing was considered very important, and we have the example of Jacob being covered with animal skin so that he might steal his father's last blessing from Esau.

Given this importance, it is curious to find that the blessing did not become universally a part of the Mass until the thirteenth century. This was because it was reserved to the Pope and Bishops, and in the large number of monastic churches where private Masses were said there was no need of a blessing.

In the new missal many other additional blessings are given for various occasions. And so the priest before departing blesses the people, as our Lord blessed them before departing at his Ascension, "He lifted up his hands and blessed them; and even as he blessed them he departed from them and was carried up to heaven." (Lk. 24:50).

Dismissal

After the blessing there is a formal dismissal. Such an announcement was quite common in ancient times at the end of any gathering. For the Mass it took on a religious form, and we now have a choice of three — all of them including the word "peace." We are sent forth into the world with love and peace in our hearts, in order to live what we have just received.

Thanks be to God

The people end by thanking God who has nourished them on the Word and on the Eucharist.

Conclusion

It is rather curious, that of all the names by which this service has been known, the one which is most common and which has remained is the word "Mass" which signifies a dismissal or departure rather than a coming together. It is from the Latin "mittere" to send away, and also from the dismissal at the end of Mass: "Ite, Missa est." The people were sent away with a laying on of hands. It is very similar today. The priest calls down the blessing of God upon the people and sends them out into the world. We have been fed on the Word of God and the Eucharist and we are dismissed or "sent out" to live the Christian message in our lives.

4

Seasons of the Church

Just as in the calendar year we have the seasons of Spring, Summer, Autumn, Winter — so in the Church year also we have seasons. In the same way that Spring leads us into Summer, and then follows Autumn — so too the seasons of the Church lead naturally from one to another. Finally, as each season has its own beauty and charm (Spring flowers or Autumn colors), so too the seasons of the Church, though very different, all have their own attraction and special message. They trace for us the life of Christ, leading up to the most important events: his death and resurrection. Because Easter is the most important feast of all, every other feast or season revolves around it. Whenever Mass is offered, it is the death and resurrection of Christ that is celebrated. Easter is at the very center of the Church year because the Risen Christ is at the center of our faith.

The Church year was not something planned from the very beginning; it just grew. It began with Easter as the only feast, but by the second century this had been extended to a time of celebration after Easter. This expanded into a Paschal cycle of feasts, both before and after Easter, which later lead to the appearance of Lent as a period of preparation. Next came the observance of Christmas and around this there also grew up a Christmas cycle, of both preparation before (Advent) and celebration afterwards — Christmas octave and Epiphany.

In the remaining time, which belonged neither to one or to the other, a number of memorial days were introduced, chiefly feasts of saints. It wasn't until the twelfth century that the sum total of all feasts together throughout the year were regarded as having any kind of unity. It was at this time that Advent was taken as the beginning of the Church year, although it had made its appearance long before, so that we start by preparing for the birth of Christ. This brings us to the feast of Christmas with its octave. Epiphany recalls that Christ's birth was made known to the world through the three wise men. Lent prepares us for his passion and death, and resurrection. The celebration of so great a feast continues for fifty days (Paschaltide) until Christ sends the Holy Spirit to be with his Church — Pentecost. Then follow the ordinary Sundays of the year, each with its own theme unfolding to us the riches of God in Word and Sacrament as he nourishes us on our pilgrimage through life.

The colors of vestments were established by Pope Pius V in 1570; the Church speaks to us through all our senses. Purple is worn for Advent and Lent as a sign of penance and so as not to anticipate the joy of the feasts before they arrive. For this same reason we modulate our outward signs of joy at the Mass and do not have the Gloria or the Alleluia during these seasons. White and gold vestments (the colors of joy) are worn for many great feasts. Red is the color of the blood of the martyrs and of fire at Pentecost. Green is the color that we see most often on a Sunday. This is the color of nature and of the new life which shoots in the spring. It reminds us that during the Church year we are always being given new life: green is the color of hope, and the Christian goes on his pilgrim way, full of faith and hope.

Advent

I rather like the story of the small boy who returned home from the circus and was asked by his father which part was the most exciting. He replied, "The part at the beginning, just before it all started." We all know exactly what he meant; this sense of wonderment and anticipation has been delightfully recaptured in Renoir's famous painting of a young girl sitting in a box at the Opera for the first time, wide-eyed with excitement, waiting for it all to start. This is how we ought to feel as Advent begins. As adults in a technological and often violent age, we tend to lose the sense of awe and wonderment and discovery that children have. Advent is a time to recapture something of this spirit.

And so the Church begins on a note of joyful and vigilant expectancy and longing. Anticipation is half the pleasure of an event, and there is an old saying that it is better to travel hopefully than to arrive. We go about our work with a deep quiet joy as we look forward to some happy event, as expressed in Isaiah: "You heavens, rain down the just one!" (Isaiah 45:8). The parched earth becomes a symbol of a parched people longing for God, or, as the psalmist says, "As the deer yearns for running streams, so my soul is yearning for you, my God." (Psalm 41).

The idea of waiting in anticipation and hope is conveyed in the bible by such people as Isaiah, Zachary, Elizabeth, Anna, Simeon and John the Baptist. The fulfilment of the promise is sure but there is a time of waiting and it is up to us how we use it.

The word "Advent" means "coming" and it is a preparation for 1) Christ's birth at Christmas, 2) his coming into our hearts, 3) his coming at the end of time, when all things will be brought to completion.

The Church recalls the approach of the Lord. The liturgy does not just recall the past — it deals with events that are still relevant for us today. Advent summons us to a preparation which we all need to make, so that Christ may be born more fully into our lives. The Church does this through the three great prophets of Advent: Isaiah, John the Baptist and our Lady. There is the famous call in chapter 40 of Isaiah, "Straighten the way of the Lord." It is a summons to men to make things straight, more particularly to make a straight way whereby the Lord may enter their hearts. Straightness is an almost universal symbol for what is right and good, as is crookedness for what is wrong and evil.

The second great figure of Advent is John the Baptist; the theme of his preaching is conversion. He brings us a cleansing rite, a public act, a symbolic immersion to make us clean. He challenges men and women, if they want to enter the Kingdom, to undergo that fundamental change of inner attitude and outward behavior which is implied in repentance. This finds its expression in baptism, and this mystical death to one's old self is the first step in the Christian life. One can think of repentance as an external act of penance or as an internal attitude but really it is both. It means an inner change so radical that one's whole way of life is also changed. The repentance John preached always remains the way into the Kingdom and he is always relevant, since he calls for a preparation that all need to make.

Finally, as we approach Christmas, our Lady comes into

focus. She represents the actual event and presents Christ to us. She too awaits his coming, both within her womb and in faith (Luke 1:45).

The season has four Sundays. It is an ancient custom to have an Advent wreath with four candles and to light them according to the Sunday, so heralding the approach of the King of Light. Throughout the season is a spirit of joy, hope and expectancy as we prepare to celebrate the birth of our Savior.

Christmas

As I mentioned in the first chapter, it often comes as quite a surprise to some people to learn that December 25th is probably not the date of the birth of Christ! Since the actual date of his birth is unknown, Christians chose a symbolic date, that of the winter solstice with its reference to the returning sun; Christ's birth was a new dawn that brought light to our darkened world. There was nothing unusual in this, as Greeks and Romans often chose to celebrate the birthdays of rulers and famous men on days other than the actual date. The Romans began their Saturnalia in mid-December, hanging up laurels and evergreens as decoration, and this custom spread throughout the territories they occupied. We still use evergreen to make our Advent wreaths and to decorate our homes and churches — symbol of immortality. And so this ancient winter solstice festival in honor of the Sun came to be observed in honor of the birth of Christ. The first account of it goes back to the year 336.

The feast of Christmas is considered second only to Easter and has its own octave, with various feasts of the infancy such as the Holy Family. On Christmas Day the Pope offered three Masses, midnight, dawn and daytime, and it became customary for all priests to do the same.

The texts of these three Masses reflect something of the time of day they are celebrated.

In the humblest possible circumstances and in total obscurity, a child was born who was to transform human life, thought, values and history and thereby create a great religion and a great civilisation. I doubt if there was any birth in the world seemingly so insignificant and yet there has never been a birth more significant. On that day, God came down to earth to live among men as a man, in due course to die, thereby abolishing death forever. By dying, he showed men how to live.

All the arts have combined to tell this wonderful event. Sometimes they have sentimentalized it, but they have tried to recapture something of the awe and wonder and love of this man and show it in the Christ-child; and they do convey something of the transcendence of God, of the one who is so "wholly other."

Christ's birth is not just an event of the past. We must be mindful of his continuous presence. Just as he showed himself to his mother and the shepherds and enlightened the magi, so he is addressing human beings in all ages and every place until the end of time. It is the birth of this child and the proclamation of his teaching that has transformed lives and shaped civilisations for the last two thousand years. Among much else that Christmas tells us is its reminder of the presence of God in the world, offering us a new birth, a new joy, a new hope.

Epiphany

It would seem that the origin of the feast of the Epiphany is similar to that of Christmas: in Egypt a feast of the winter solstice was celebrated on January 6th. The word "epiphany" comes from the Greek, meaning manifestation or appearance and in the East it came to mean the appearing of Christ, King of Light, in this world. The feast spread to the West in the fourth century and was linked with the visit of the three wise men or magi recorded in the Gospels. The word "magus" means a priest of member or a priestly class in ancient Persia. Christ was born in obscurity but made himself known to the world through the three wise men. There must have been times on their journey when the star was not clearly visible. But they kept faith with the light that had been shown to them. To many of us today God seems hidden; pressures to which we are exposed make it difficult for us to believe, but the light still shines in the darkness and we, in turn, must offer our fellow men a focus of faith to live by.

During this season we also have the feast of the Baptism of Christ and of the miracle at Cana — both signs of Christ's divinity. In fact, the Sundays after the Epiphany are dominated by epiphany-thoughts such as miracles by which Christ manifested his divine power and texts in praise of the God-King. They could be summed up by the words of the Gospel on the second Sunday, which recounts the miracle of Cana: "He let his glory be seen and his disciples believed in him." (John 1:11). The feast of the Presentation of our Lord on February 2nd (Candlemas Day) completes the Christmas cycle forty days after it began.

Lent

The idea of preceding Easter with a fast of forty days, just as Christ fasted forty days in the desert, originated as far back as the fourth century. Even before this it had been customary to fast on a few days before the great feast. Since there are six Sundays in a Lent of forty days, and one never fasted on a Sunday which was always a day of joy in honor of the Risen Christ, there were only thirty-four actual fastdays. To make up the full forty the Church included Good Friday and Holy Saturday and the four days before the first Sunday of Lent. This is how Lent came to begin on Ash Wednesday. Fasting meant having one meal, which would be in the evening, and abstaining from flesh meat and from wine. With fasting went voluntary almsgiving. People undertook to do these two things in order to strengthen their prayers, to do penance for their sins, to help the poor, and as a self-discipline in preparation for Easter. Gradually what was voluntary became obligatory and by the Middle Ages various rules were fixed. Before the evening meal the people would gather at a "stational" (any of the major churches in Rome) church where the priest celebrated Mass. They would go to the church in procession, singing litanies.

During the season of Lent there were three main themes: Baptism (those baptised were instructed during Lent and it is a suitable time to renew our baptismal commitment); Penance (conversion back to God); and the Passion of our Lord. The readings on the third and fourth Sundays still recall such themes as water, the blind man who sees again, and the dead who are raised to life.

Public penitents were excluded from Holy Communion during this time (they could still attend Mass clad in hair shirts!) and were formally received back at the Mass of the Lord's Supper on Maundy Thursday. This day was so called because of the new "mandatum" or command we received from our Lord on that evening, to love one another. During the seventh century public penitents were banned altogether from the Church during Lent, as our first parents were banned from the Garden of Eden. The same words from the book of Genesis were used, "Remember, man, that thou art dust. . . ." and a special blessing was given and ashes imposed before they departed. After a few centuries everyone received ashes, thereby acknowledging sinfulness and need for conversion during Lent.

The whole emphasis of Lent is on "conversion," meaning a turning around, a change of heart. The prophet Joel reminds us on Ash Wednesday, "It is your hearts that must be broken, not your garments torn." (Joel 2:12). This involves the destruction and mystical death of the "old man" in order that the "new man," the image of Christ, may be born in us.

As Holy Week draws near, the emphasis moves to the Passion of Christ, and very early on they had a procession with palms to commemorate Christ's entry into Jerusalem. On Maundy Thursday morning the Bishop celebrated Mass, as he still does, with all his clergy to consecrate the oils for anointing those to be received into the church at Easter. In the evening the priests of each parish celebrate together the Mass of the Lord's Supper. In the cathedral and in some churches there is the "mandatum" or washing of feet, done by Christ at the Last Supper as an example of service to others. After Mass "the watch" continues until midnight, in memory of Christ and his apostles praying in the Garden of Gethsemane.

On Good Friday the service is in three parts — prayers and readings, as in the first part of the Mass, veneration of the cross, which takes the place of the sacrificial action of the Mass, and lastly a Communion service.

The Easter Vigil on Holy Saturday is the greatest event in the whole of the Church year. It is a festival of light and of water. The first part is centered around the blessing of the new fire (this was done each day by the monks who needed the light for reciting Vespers) and then the blessing of the Paschal candle, symbol of the Risen Christ. The Candle is borne through the darkened church and we light our candles from it, to show how the light of the Risen

Christ must spread to the whole world. The priest then sings the "Exultet," a song of welcome to the newly Risen Christ.

The second part is centered around the blessing of the baptismal water, to be used for those who are to be baptized. The lessons recall how water in the bible is a sign of life and of death. The people of God passed through the Red Sea, which brought them to new life and freedom from slavery; it brought death to the Egyptians. Christ died on the cross to overcome sin and death, and rose to a new life. Through baptism we also renounce evil and begin to share God's life. As the lesson reminds us, "When we were baptized in Christ Jesus we were baptized in his death; in other words, when we were baptized we went into the tomb with him and joined him in death, so that as Christ was raised from the dead by the Father's glory, we too might live a new life." (Romans 6:3 and 4). We renew once again our baptismal promises, and having done battle against the "old self" during Lent, we come to a joyful celebration of the feast of the Risen Christ.

Easter

It is interesting for us to discover that for the first three centuries in the history of the Church, Easter was the only feast celebrated. Everything revolved around the resurrection, "If Christ be not risen, then we are still in our sins and our believing is vain." (Cor. 15:17). Today there is great discussion about a fixed date for Easter. We still use the Jewish reckoning for fixing the date, and the Jews divided the year into lunar months, each beginning with the new moon. The Pasch was always on the fourteenth day of the Spring month. At the end of the second century Pope Victor decided that Easter should be celebrated everywhere on the Sunday that followed the Spring full moon, because this is a time when we celebrate new life. This is brought out very clearly in the poem of Francis Thompson called "Ode to the Setting Sun:"

The fall doth pass the rise in worth;
For birth hath in itself the germ of death,
But death hath in itself the germ of life.
It is the falling acorn buds the tree,
The falling rain that bears the greenery,
The fern-plants moulder when the ferns arise.
For there is nothing lives but something dies,
And there is nothing dies but something lives,
Till skies be fugitives.

We see resurrection going on all the time in the world of nature — it is the pattern of God's creation. Plants die, and live again in the seeds which are dispersed in their death; even universes die, as new stars are born from the dust of the old. And Easter is the month when we discover that this happens for us too. Life comes out of suffering and death. From sharing Christ's suffering and death, we come to share his resurrection. If Good Friday goes on all the time — so does Easter!

Easter was celebrated during the night, because it was during the night leading to Easter that our Lord rose again. There were readings and prayers leading up to the Eucharist, as in the other Vigils. Baptism, the sacrament of new birth, was administered on this special night, and the ceremonies of blessing the new fire and of the large Easter candle preceded it in order to bring out this idea of new life, a sign for those who were to be enlightened by Christ. Readings from scripture led up to baptism, and then it was all concluded with a glorious celebration of the Mass of the Resurrection. It is said that the Emperor Constantine, on Easter night, caused the whole city to be illuminated with torches, so turning night into day.

The importance of Easter was emphasized by its octave, a continuation of the feast. People were free from work on these days, and gathered for Mass in the early morning and again for a service in the baptistry in the afternoon. It all ended on the Sunday after Easter which was known as Low Sunday (as opposed to High-day or Easter Day) when they wore their baptismal robes for the last time. It is from this association with baptism that we have had, from the ninth century onward, the "Asperges" or sprinkling with water at the principal Mass each Sunday, the day of new life and new birth, to remind us of our Christian baptism.

As far back as the second century people observed not only the first week after Easter as something special but also the following seven weeks. This is "Paschaltide" — ending on Pentecost Sunday when Christ sent the Holy Spirit down upon the Church. As we prepared for Easter with the forty days of Lent, so we celebrate for a further forty days the Resurrection until the Ascension; and the coming of the Holy Spirit after ten days of waiting. Eastertide is a kind of continuous celebration of Easter, and St. Athanasius called this season "the Great Sunday." During this time all fasting was at an end and people stood up to pray (instead of kneeling) as all were risen with Christ. In this season we read in the Gospels about the different appearances of the Risen Christ. He is put before us as the "Good Shepherd" who gave his life for his sheep. This image is to be found in the catacombs, and in the fifth century mosaics in Ravenna. The theme of peace is put before us on the sixth Sunday, since on his appearances Christ always greeted his apostles with the words, "Peace be with you."

Two days stand out in particular — Ascension Day and Pentecost Sunday. Ascension Day is preceded by three Rogation days or days of special petition to Christ before he ascends back to the Father. They originated in a time of severe famine in Gaul in the fifth century. At Pentecost the paschal candle is removed from the sanctuary and placed next to the Font.

But this is not the end of everything. In a unique way Easter belongs both to the past and to the present. To the past because it did happen on a given day and at a certain time and place. To the present because Christ once risen is ever alive and each one of us can know him personally. It is significant that the disciples did not recognize him at first; it took them some time to realize who he was. This is a further proof of the reality of the resurrection: it was not a vision created by their imagination. But, more importantly, it shows the newness of the Risen Lord. He is the new creation in our midst. To come into contact with him we need a new mode of perception which belongs to the new creation. This is faith.

We must read the story of Christ's life backwards, and then it makes sense. Christian belief begins with the resurrection, which throws its light backwards upon the death and ministry that went before and so illuminates all the paradoxes. Our Easter joy comes from the conviction that Christ has entered our world, has died, has risen and lives among us still. During Easter and after it is over may we rejoice in the company of the Risen Christ and, transformed by Easter faith, go about our lives with deep joy. May these words of St. Augustine find an echo in our hearts: "We are Easter men and 'Alleluia' is our Easter song."

Pentecost

At the feast of Pentecost we celebrate two important things:
1. The completion of the work of redemption by the outpouring of the Holy Spirit.
2. The birth of the Church.

The word means "fiftieth" day after Easter. On this day God sent down the Holy Spirit upon his Church and so completed the wonderful events of our redemption. The word "Spirit" means breath or life. In the Old Testament the Spirit means originally the movement of air, the breath or the wind. It is the principle of life and of vital activity present at the time of creation; "And God's Spirit hovered over the water . . ." In creation the Spirit brought order out of chaos and light out of darkness. (Gen. 1:2). The wind is the breath of God and the Spirit is a dynamic force. Just as it is difficult to trace the origin and course of the wind, so it is with the Spirit. As Christ said to Nicodemus, "The wind blows wherever it pleases, you hear its sound, but you cannot tell where it comes from or where it is going. That is how it is with all who are born of the Spirit." (John 3:8).

We can witness the transformation produced in someone by the Spirit, but we cannot explain it: a power that moves a man to do that which is normally impossible for him and to rise above his own capacities. We note for example the Judges of Israel who were helped by the Spirit in their work, and the Kings, who after being anointed received the Spirit to help them to rule. The Prophets, too, were assisted by the Spirit, for the charisma of the prophet is the Word, "The Spirit of the Lord is upon me, he has anointed me, and sent me to bring good news to men." (Isaiah 61:1). An important aspect of the vocation of a prophet was to revive hope. In the valley of dry bones (Ezechiel 37), you have a picture of the defeat of a nation and a Church (Israel was both), but the Spirit of God breathes new life and hope into them. We, too, are renewed and re-created by the Spirit.

Spirit, then, is hard to define and we recognize it best at work: a rather mysterious divine force or impulse, God at work in His own way. When our Lord was about to leave the apostles, he told them that he would not leave them friendless but would send them the Holy Spirit, who would not only be constantly at their side but would dwell within them. In this way Christ reaches man's innermost being and changes him from within. We must be guided by the Spirit rather than by nature. (Gal. 5).

The apostolic group had to carry out the mission of Jesus, but they were unable to do so until they had received the Spirit. After Pentecost they were transformed, and showed eloquence and courage in great contrast to their former slowness and timidity. When threatened by the authorities, who were astonished at their "boldness," they replied, "It is impossible for us to refrain from speaking of what we have seen and heard." (Acts 4:21). The divine impulse compelled them to go forward, just as Jesus himself was "led" by the Spirit. (Matt. 4:1).

We too have received the Holy Spirit in our lives and can feel the same renewal and transformation. In the early Church confirmation used to be given immediately after baptism. Since baptism commits us to the Christian way of life and makes us members of the Christian family, confirmation helps and inspires us in this commitment and to play our part in the community. The feast of Pentecost is the celebration of the Holy Spirit in the lives of those who follow Christ. It is succeeded on the next Sunday by the feast of the Holy Trinity, as a kind of summing up of all that has been done for mankind by the Father, Son and Holy Spirit.

I have said that the feast of Pentecost also marked the actual birth of the Church. It was from the time of the first Pentecost that the Church began to expand. Peter went out and preached to the multitudes, and "about three thousand souls were won for the Lord that day." (Acts 2:42). We all help in the work of building up the Church. "To each one is given the manifestation of the Spirit for a good purpose." (1 Cor. 12:7). The manifestations of the Holy Spirit or charisms are different gifts of the Spirit, given to each to help in the work. At Pentecost the Church began her earthly pilgrimage which will be completed only at the end of time.

Sundays of the Year

The thirty three or four Sundays which are outside the Christmas and Easter cycles are called "Sundays of the Year." They represent our earthly pilgrimage to God, until we come round to celebrate again the beginning of the Church year at Advent. During these Sundays there is no over-all theme, but the lectionary arranges the New Testament texts for semi-continuous reading, taking us through the "rich treasury" of the bible. The Gospel readings fit into a pattern so that the early Sundays tell of the early preaching and ministry of Christ after his baptism, while the later ones take our minds forward to the end of time. The Old Testament lesson is usually chosen to harmonize with the Gospel and show how many events of the New Testament were foreshadowed in the Old.

Feasts of Saints

From very early on in her history, the Church began to venerate the saints. She did this out of the knowledge that they were with Christ, and their example and prayers have great power for us. Because Easter and Christmas are the two great feasts of the year, saints are associated with either the Easter cycle or the Christmas cycle.

Easter Cycle

We find many examples of people in the ancient world keeping the anniversaries of their dead. There was nothing unusual therefore in Christians doing this, and they would observe the anniversary by celebrating the Eucharist. Because of the early persecutions, some of the first to be venerated after emerging from the catacombs were the martyrs. Easter would seem to be the most appropriate time for celebrating these, drawing a parallel between their victory over suffering and death and the triumph of Christ. Later, saints who were not martyrs were added to the Easter cycle.

Finally it became impossible to devote a feast day to each saint, and there were days for groups of martyrs and then for all those who had no feast day of their own. This feast of All Saints used to be on May 13th, very clearly within the Easter season. It was Gregory IV in 835 who transferred it to November 1st. It still comes well before the last Sunday of the Church year, which is dedicated to Christ the King — symbolizing the Paschal idea of the victory and eternal reign of Christ.

Christmas Cycle

The greatest of all the saints is Mary and because of her place in the Incarnation at Christmas she has her own feast on January 1st, "the Solemnity of Mary, Mother of God." Other great feasts of Our Lady — her Birthday, the Annunciation and her Assumption — were introduced into Rome about the seventh century. They all originated in the East. It was natural that after Arius had cast doubts on the divinity of Christ, this divinity should have been stressed. In so doing, the reverence due to his mother was also emphasized, giving rise to these feasts.

Other feasts take their bearings from scripture. John the Baptist for example had his feast fixed on June 24th, six months before the birth of Christ, since his mother Elizabeth was "already in her sixth month," (Luke 1:36) when she was visited by Mary. The feast of the Annunciation is on March 25th, nine months before Christmas.

In early times the keeping of feast days was up to the local church. Each community had its local saints or saints connected with its order. Only feasts of general importance were observed by the whole Church. Gradually a distinction grew up between holidays of obligation, which would to some extent affect civil life, and other feasts observed by the monks in choir. By the Middle Ages there were no fewer than forty-three holidays of obligation apart from Sundays, together with a few proper to each diocese. They were reduced in 1642 to thirty-three, and by 1917 there were only ten. Today there are seven. In the early Church the important feasts had a vigil the night before, with readings, prayers and fasting. Now the three principal feasts have a vigil — Easter, Christmas and Pentecost, and also the important feasts of St. John the Baptist, Ss. Peter and Paul, and the Assumption. In the renewal that our calendar has undergone recently, the Church has tried to make it universal both geographically (all five continents are now represented) and chronologically (the choir of saints covers the whole period of the Church's history). An effort has been made to authenticate the lives of the early saints, and where this has not been possible, they have disappeared from the calendar. A diocese or religious order may have a supplement to the Church's calendar, which allows them to celebrate locally holy men and women who have lived and served in that area.

Conclusion

All these feasts and seasons have a commemorative character, but not in the usual sense only. In civil acts of commemoration and remembrance (such as Remembrance Sunday around the village war memorial), we recall events by words and action. It is not just in this way that the Church commemorates. When we celebrate a feast or a mystery the event is brought in a mysterious manner from the past into the present, not in itself but in its effects and in its source. What we celebrate is not just a representation of past events — it is something alive, having its effects here and now.

5

Art and Liturgy
What to look for in a
Church

Early Christian art goes right back to the catacombs, where you find on the walls symbols such as fish and loaves, or a fish on its own. The five letters of the word "fish" in Greek are the same as the letters beginning each of the words (written above the cross), "Jesus Christ, Son of God, Savior;" hence the meaning of a fish in Christian symbolism.

Long before this time the psalmist had written the words, "Lord, I have loved the beauty of thy house and the place where thy glory dwelleth." (Ps.9 26:8).

In the fourth century, as soon as Christians moved out of the catacombs and began building basilicas to house their growing numbers, there followed the baptism of architecture, painting, sculpture, music and letters in the service and praise of God. Throughout the centuries, man offers to God the greatest beauty he has, and the fine arts are considered to rank among the noblest expressions of human genius. The aim of such art is to turn men's thoughts to God and to serve his honor and glory. All things that are set aside for divine worship should be truly worthy, and symbols of heavenly realities. They are symbols of the sacred in the midst of the secular. As the Constitution on the liturgy reminds us, "In the earthly liturgy we take part in a foretaste of that heavenly liturgy which is celebrated in the holy city of Jerusalem toward which we journeyed as pilgrims." These signs and symbols link up with something that is beyond.

Each age has engaged its very best craftsmen to build up the glory of God's house, each period has bequeathed expressions of faith in music, art, stone, glass and poetry. The Christmas story is told in different ways by Bach in his "Christmas Oratio," by Rubens in the "Adoration of the Magi" (in King's College chapel), and by Milton in his poem "On the morning of Christ's Nativity."

One of the functions of art is to mirror the culture of the age. In the glory of Gothic architecture we see how the spirit of man moved in the Middle Ages, reaching out through height and light for the transcendent. In marked contrast, the people of today prefer simple, clean outlines in the things that surround them. Those of the Baroque and Gothic periods loved complexity and detail, but they were people of simple and strong faith. Today the roles have been reversed; man himself seems more complex, and so he surrounds himself with simple, unfussy things, and hence different art forms evolve. The best of contemporary work can and must co-exist with the best of the past. Pope Paul expressed this thought when he opened the permanent museum of contemporary art at the Vatican in 1973. He spoke of modern artists, "as the poets and prophets of our times, speaking to us of man today, of his outlook and of our modern society." There is also the change in materials, style and ornamentation which the progress of the technical arts has brought.

However, in our efforts to modernize our churches, we have sometimes discarded things of real beauty that belong to the past. If we do that, beauty is no longer allowed as a handmaiden to holiness and religion can become an unlovely thing. We should be mindful not merely of modern relevance but of the timeless value of beauty. Many of the furnishings of a church were designed for and fit into that building, which was conceived as a unit with due regard for scale and style. Often, too, such things are bound up with the particular history of a local church (a font, for example) and should not lightly be cast aside. On the other hand we must be discriminating and in the words of the Vatican Council document on Sacred Art, "We must exclude those works of artists which offend true religious sense, either by their distortion of forms or their lack of artistic worth, by mediocrity or by pretence."

The word "aesthetic" comes from the Greek for "feeling" — that is why an anaesthetic is something that takes away feeling. The liturgy, literally "the work of praying," is bound to involve us aesthetically, filling time and space with the best possible expressions of our feeling. Language matters and presentation matters. In all these things the spirit of man reaches out to God. Often we can only speak in poetry and symbols, to hint at divine mysteries.

The Shape and Style of a Church

One of the most revolutionary innovations of Christianity was the fact that it did not just associate worship with

99

a certain place such as the Temple. Worship can take place wherever a holy people are gathered before God, for they themselves are the true temple of the Lord, "Do you not understand that you are God's temple, and that God's Spirit has his dwelling in you? If anybody desecrates the temple of God, God will bring him to ruin. It is a holy thing, this temple of God which is nothing other than yourselves." (1 Cor. 3:16-17). The word "Church" used to designate a building and comes from "ecclesia," which means an assembly or gathering.

There is little mention in early Christianity of a place for worship, as the people just assembled in one of their rooms. "They met in their homes for the breaking of bread." (Acts 2:46). The Eucharist was also celebrated in the burial places for the dead and on the tombs of the martyrs. From this arose the custom of placing relics in an altar stone.

When the Christians emerged from the catacombs in the fourth century, then the basilica began to take shape. As the living church is built up of priest and people, so the building is composed of Sanctuary and Nave. It is liturgical worship that must govern the architecture and not vice versa. The church building develops as an outer frame surrounding the celebration of Mass. According to ancient custom the sanctuary faces the east, the Orient, and the people's part the "nave" (from the Latin meaning "a ship") represents the people voyaging towards the east, toward the light which is God. In fact many Gothic churches with their flying buttresses very much resemble a ship.

Just as we were consecrated in baptism, which means "set aside" for God — so the building is consecrated. It is sprinkled with holy water as a type of baptism and the crosses on the walls are anointed. It is set aside for a holy purpose.

In the east the shape of a Greek cross was often used for the building, a cross with four arms of equal length, the altar being at the center where all lines converge.

In our country, after the Romans had left and the Celts stayed on, we had the Dark Ages of the fifth and sixth centuries. The Celts became Christians toward the end of the sixth century. This was when the Saxons invaded our island. The Saxon churches are the first really important architectural buildings in England. Two of the most outstanding examples are in Essex: Greenstead, still with its wooden walls, and Bradwell. The Saxons also invented parishes.

When the Normans came they built in the round arched style that was used throughout christendom, with an apse at the east end of the church for the priest's chair. This style replaced the wooden churches of the Saxons. The Normans encouraged monks and nuns to come and settle in Britain, and this is why many monasteries and also cathedrals are Norman in origin. They used to build cross-shaped buildings with central towers, designed to dominate the district. The walls were usually painted, and also the east end, in order to give the effect of the mosaics of an eastern basilica.

The origin of Gothic was the necessity to roof an oblong space with stone, as wooden roofs were liable to catch fire. One can recognize the Early English style by its acutely pointed arches and slender columns clustered together rather like pipes of stone. It was an age of great faith, and they built for the glory of God.

During the fourteenth century, architectural techniques were improving all the time and the decorated period developed. If the architecture of the Saxons and Normans was heavy and dark, Gothic architecture reached out for height and light. The decorated period was known chiefly for large windows and an abundance of sculpture and tracery. Tracery consisted of bars of stone interspersing the large windows and these bars were often richly carved.

Perpendicular architecture originated in France and lasted longer than any of the other English Gothic styles. It is a very good name for a style with tall vertical lines to support the arches and tracery in windows. Religion was strong in the lives of the people and there was a great devotion to the Mother of God. One is struck by the number of old churches that are dedicated to St. Mary the Virgin, and most Cathedrals and Churches of this period had a lady chapel. The Church was the center of the village and the center of people's lives. The Gothic style was an attempt to create a semblance of heaven on earth through stone, height, light, color and music.

After the reign of Henry VIII very few churches were built; instead, large country houses sprang up, sometimes from the ruins of the monasteries. These houses often had features found in the Gothic churches, such as large mullioned windows, large halls with open roofs, dining halls with wooden screens and panelling. After their death the owners of these houses were commemorated in the parish church by elaborate and splendid monuments in marble or stone.

This led on to a revival of the architecture of ancient Rome as expressed in the Renaissance style. One of the greatest architects of the new style was Sir Christopher Wren, who carefully adapted it to incorporate something of the Gothic style that had gone before. After the Great Fire of London in 1666 he was put in charge of rebuilding many of the churches in the city. He carefully designed the height of his churches and steeples to lead the eye to the greatest of his works, the dome of St. Paul's.

In the nineteenth century there was a revival of the Gothic with architects like Barry and Pugin. They worked together on the Houses of Parliament and Pugin went on to build many well known Catholic churches in the Victorian Gothic style. The most famous of these is St. Chad's Cathedral in Birmingham. At about the same time Sir Gilbert Scott built or restored a vast number of churches in the Decorated Gothic style. A lot of small country churches were also built in this style. At the end of the century John Bentley built Westminster Cathedral in the Byzantine style, with red brick and bands of white Portland stone. The interior gives an uninterrupted view of the high altar and is impressive in its size and with a strong feeling of mystery and of the holy.

After the revivals we have churches constructed in the new materials of glass, concrete and steel. One of the chief influences in this new style was the French architect le Corbusier who, during the 1930s, was already designing simple but impressive, inspired churches on the continent in this way. Imaginative use is made of reinforced concrete (as in the underground basilica in Lourdes) and emphasis is laid upon simplicity and the function of the building. This is seen in the cathedral of Christ the King in Liverpool, where the function of the building — to house the altar and the people — dictates the style and shape of the building.

While many of the Cathedrals and Churches built in the past styles I have been describing are beautiful in themselves, they are not always very satisfactory for carrying out the liturgy. In a long Gothic church, for example, the length of the nave makes it difficult both to see and to take part. The plan of any building does or should depend primarily upon its purpose, and for a church this means making adequate provision for the sacred liturgy and for those who take part in it, the clergy. choir and congregation. As the General Instruction on the Roman Missal says, "The people of God, when assembled for Mass, has an organic and hierarchical structure which is manifested in the various actions and different functions performed during the Mass. Hence the shape of the church ought in some way to suggest the form of the assembly and the different functions of its members." (G.I. 275). The church must be so designed as to allow the celebration of the liturgy "according to its true nature" and to secure the active participation of the people.

Many of our older churches have had to be adapted. Such a matter should be done with great feeling and consideration both for the liturgy and for the building. One must always be guided by certain liturgical principles as each part and object of the building is considered. When buildings are an expression of a certain period they should not be remodelled to look like something else. There is no need to destroy their character when a little sensitive planning can both adapt them to modern needs and preserve all that is good in them. As I said in the beginning, many of the original fittings of a church may be adapted and re-used for our liturgy today. This has the advantage of retaining things that have gone to make up the homogeneity of the building and have become part of its history.

Altar

There should be two chief focal points in any church: the altar, on which the sacrifice is accomplished, and the lectern for the liturgy of the Word. The altar is in the Sanctuary, the "holy" part of the church, itself distinguished from the rest of the church by some feature such as a raised floor, special shape or decoration. The altar should be made of natural stone and be free-standing. Early altars were made of wood, but in 1076 the Council of Winchester decreed that where possible the altar should be made of stone. It should be in such a position that the entire congregation naturally focus their attention upon it. The word "altar" means in Latin the "high point."

In the very earliest days of church building, an effort was always made to set up the altar in such a way that it seemed to belong to both nave and choir. It was placed at the intersection of the two with the priest facing the people. In the early Middle Ages, in an attempt to express the sacredness and aloofness of the mystery, it was moved to the east wall. At the same time the choir was increased in size and a screen marked the end of it. Sometimes there were rather heavy screens designed to separate the clergy, not the altar, from the people. When, however, the altar was put near the east wall, the wall itself was decorated with Christian symbols such as Christ the good Shepherd, the Lamb of God, or Christ with the apostles and saints. A large reredos or screen was erected behind the altar with perhaps a painting of the saint of the church on it. Massive altars developed in which the "mensa" or table part was almost lost. A baldachino or canopy was often placed over the altar, or the ceiling above was painted, to mark it out as a place of honor.

We ourselves are the living temple of God and are consecrated with oil at our baptism; the altar when it is consecrated is anointed with oil on the five crosses incised on the table of sacrifice in memory of the five wounds of Christ. It is covered with a cloth as befits a table and has candles.

From the thirteenth century onward there was a large increase in the number of private Masses. More altars were required and these were ranged in side chapels around the choir.

In the new Order of Mass the church emphasizes that the altar is both the table of sacrifice and the Lord's table from which the people are nourished. Accordingly it has been brought back from the east wall and stands at the most focal point, where sanctuary and nave meet; all may gather around, see clearly and take part in the communal celebration of the Eucharist. Everything should converge at this point. The lines of the building, the light from the stained glass lantern, the pattern of the floor, and the baldachino suspended over the altar, all proclaim it to be the focal point.

It should be very much the focal point rather than the central point. Round churches with central altars can provide more liturgical problems than they solve and are unsatisfactory when it comes to proclaiming the scriptures and preaching. The whole building must be arranged so that there is an intelligent and sympathetic ordering of its interior space, which directs people toward what is going on and helps them to participate in it.

Lectern

The whole of the first part of the Mass is centered around the liturgy of the Word. According to the General Instruction on the Roman Missal, "The dignity of God's Word requires that some fitting place be provided whence it may be proclaimed; it should be a place on which people naturally concentrate their attention during the liturgy of the Word." (G.I. 272). The importance given to the book and the lectern express our belief that God is present among us and speaks to us through his Word.

We have seen the importance given to the Word in the Jewish synagogue service from which the first part of our Mass derives. As far back as the fifth century B.C., it is recorded in Nehemiah 8.4 that, "Ezra the scribe stood upon a pulpit of wood which they had made for the purpose." In the early Christian church, as soon as buildings were constructed, there is mention of an elevated place in churches where the reading desk, ambo or pulpit stood for the presentation of the sacred text. Some were moveable and made of wood, bronze or brass; others were of marble or stone and in later times richly decorated. Lecterns in the form of an eagle with open wings (symbol of St. John the Evangelist) became popular in the thirteenth and fourteenth centuries. Brass lecterns of the seventeenth century can be seen in the college chapels of Oxford and Cambridge. Those in parish churches usually date from the Victorian period. Often a pulpit had a sounding board above to help project the voice, and an hour glass so that the preacher should know when to stop! At a time when long sermons were fashionable, the pulpit was often placed in the body of the church so that the preacher could be seen as well as heard.

In our renewed liturgy importance is given again to this center of the Word. It is the center of proclamation as used by the reader and priest. If possible, the lectern should be on the right of the altar (when facing the congregation) in the place of honor. It may be made of the same material as the altar to show the relation between the two. As St. Hilary wrote, in the fourth century, "It is at the table of the Lord that we receive our nourishment, the Bread of Life; but it is at the table of the readings that we are nourished by the teaching of the Lord."

Celebrant's Chair

The celebrant's chair draws attention to his function of presiding over the community and leading its prayer. The proper place for it is at the apex of the sanctuary, facing the people. For the first few centuries it was the seat of the Bishop and the Bishop himself was the center of the Mass, as it was he who offered up the Eucharist to God. The wooden altar was carried in by deacons when required. The throne or presiding chair remained in a central position in the apse of the church until the Middle Ages. In Norwich cathedral the eleventh century stone throne is still in its original position. But during the Middle Ages, when the altar was moved to the east wall, the throne or chair was placed at the side. In old churches the three sedilia (as they are called in Latin) may still be seen on the right hand side as you face the altar, recessed into the wall, where the three priests would sit when celebrating High Mass. Now that the altar is once again facing the people, the chair may be placed in its original presiding position at the apex of the sanctuary.

Christ is present in the Eucharist and in the Word at Mass, and also in the minister who presides and in the people who gather together. "Where two or three are gathered together in my name, I am there in the midst of them." (Matt. 18:20). When the Bishop lays hands on one to be ordained, he declares that he is ordaining him for three purposes — to sacrifice, to preach and to preside. The last function is signified by the presiding chair. In this position the priest is seen to be presiding as a father over a family, and leading them in prayer.

Tabernacle

This word comes from the Latin meaning a tent. In the book of Exodus we read how Moses pitched a tent outside the camp and called it the tent of meeting, and everyone who sought the Lord would go there. The Ark of the Covenant, a box lined with gold and containing the tables of God's law, was placed in the tent. God was present among his people through his Word and his presence was localized in this form.

God is with us in many ways; since the New Testament he is with us under the appearances of bread and wine which through the Mass have become his Body and Blood.

It is under this form that we have the reservation of the Blessed Sacrament in the tabernacle, with a lamp burning as a mark of reverence before the real presence. In the early days of Christianity, persecution rendered the reservation of the consecrated host impossible except occasionally in the homes of the faithful. After the persecutions, from the fourth century, the Blessed Sacrament was kept in the churches. For sixteen hundred years there was no uniformity of practice and many different customs were followed. Sometimes it was enclosed in a dove-shaped receptacle suspended before the altar or in an ordinary suspended pyx and canopy. The pyx was so sacred that it was prohibited from theft by hostile armies. In Shakespeare's "Henry V" the king delays his army for a whole day to discover who had stolen one. Henry VII left in his will a pyx to the value of ten dollars to any parish church that did not have a suitable one.

Sometimes the Blessed Sacrament was kept in a "sacrament house," a form of tabernacle either projecting from the wall of the sanctuary or on a pillar. This was very common in Germany, where examples may still be found today. Sometimes the place of reservation was in the sacristy or in an aumbry in the wall of the sanctuary.

From the sixteenth century it became common, and from the seventeenth century obligatory, to reserve the Blessed Sacrament in a tabernacle set in the middle of the altar. So it remained, until free-standing altars and Mass facing the people made this difficult. In view of this, and so that the priest could preside once again from the original position with his back to the east wall, facing the people, former ways of reserving the Blessed Sacrament were once again considered. These took into account the two main reasons for reservation: (1) for private prayer, (2) in order to be able to bring Holy Communion to the sick. Also, the priest on occasions may require more hosts for

Holy Communion. Accordingly, an instruction was issued from Rome which said, "It is strongly recommended that the Blessed Sacrament be reserved in a special chapel well suited for private prayer, apart from the nave. But if the plan of the church or legitimate local custom impedes this, then the Sacrament should be kept on an altar or elsewhere in the church suitably adorned." (G.I. 276).

Font

One of the most important features in any church is the font. In many old churches it is near the main entrance, to remind us that it was through the waters of baptism that we entered the community of Christians.

There is evidence that in the earliest days a new Christian was baptized in a river or in the sea. He was immersed or he bent down while the minister poured the water three times over his head and said the baptismal words.

Later baptism took place in the house; it was in houses that both baptism and the Eucharist were celebrated. In the third century, when the persecutions were over and large numbers were being received into the church, separate buildings called baptisteries were constructed near the churches. Many examples may still be seen in Italy today. In the center of the baptistery was a large well of water, and rooms for changing around the sides. The walls were decorated with marble and paintings or mosaics of the Good Shepherd or the hart who pants after running streams or scenes from the baptism of Christ.

The most primitive shape of the font was quadrilateral. This shape was adopted since in baptism the believer is buried with Christ, and so the font was given the form of a coffin. As St. Paul says, "You have been taught that when we were baptised in Christ Jesus we were baptised in his death; in other words, when we were baptised we went into the tomb with him and joined him in death, so that as Christ was raised from the dead by the Father's glory, we too might live a new life." (Romans 6:3).

The Saxon fonts of this country (of which hardly any examples still exist) were usually a kind of tub-shape; the Norman fonts were usually square though a few were cruciform. All these shapes derived from the idea of being buried with Christ.

From the thirteenth century onward, fonts were either hexagonal or octagonal. The hexagonal shape represents the sixth day, the day of Christ's death. The transition to the octagonal shape recalls the eighth day, the day of Christ's Resurrection. I spoke about this in the first chapter, when I said how Sunday used to be known as the eighth day — after seven days of material creation came spiritual creation, with Christ's resurrection. We begin to share this new risen life of Christ in baptism. That is why baptisms take place on a Sunday, the day of the resurrection, the first day of the week. The Christian is at a new beginning.

Eight-sided fonts sometimes pictured the seven sacraments with the eighth side often showing a scene of the crucifixion or the baptism of Christ. Importance was given to the font by raising it up, often on three steps in memory of the three days Christ spent in the tomb. In the thirteenth century font covers were added to keep the water clean and to prevent it being taken away. These became very elaborate and were beautifully carved.

Today baptism, like most sacraments, is administered usually during Mass. This is so that we can prepare for the sacrament by the liturgy of the Word and follow it by the celebration of the Eucharist. For this reason, and because the community so gathered welcomes a new member into God's family, the font today is usually somewhere toward the front of the church where it may be seen by everybody. During the year the paschal candle stands next to it, symbolizing the risen Christ whose life we share. He is the "first born out of death" and through our baptism we too have undergone death and are born again of water and the Holy Spirit.

Choir

In our revised liturgy the same principle is always insisted on: the liturgy is the celebration of a community and each group in this community has its part to play. This is especially so with the choir (and with the organ) which has to be related to both the sanctuary and the people. I have already spoken about the function of the choir, which is to lead the singing and provide the occasional anthem. The place of the choir varies more than anything else in the church, according to the architectural layout. If, however, the choir is to lead the congregation, it should not be separated from them in a choir loft at the back of the church, but should be part of the body of the church. Each must work out the best position so that both choir and organ can carry out their liturgical function and take a full active part in the mass.

Nave

This is the people's part of the church, and as I have mentioned before, the word comes from the Latin, meaning a ship. We are on a journey through life; the nave faces east, and we journey toward the heavenly light and the kingdom of God.

In early days the nave was very much the people's part of the church, and as a large building in the center of the village it was used by them for sacred plays, elections, courts and meetings. This part of the church would be quite clear since benches did not become common until the fifteenth century, when sermons became longer! Until then there were just a few stone benches around the walls, hence the expression: "the weakest goes to the wall." The box-like pews came later on, to keep out the draughts!

The nave of a large church was lit mainly from the "clear storey" windows above, which also threw light on the lovely timbered roof. Plain glass was introduced into this country in the seventh century and colored glass about the twelfth. Stained glass was greatly improved in the fifteenth century, when a yellow stain was discovered which made the tints softer and less intense. The figures and scenes depicted were a way of teaching the people their religious history, just as the sculpture on the west door of a cathedral was meant to be "sermons in stone."

At the top of the nave was the screen, which was an English version of the iconostasis of the Orthodox church. It separated the sanctuary and the clergy from the people's part. On the top of the screen was the "rood," the Crucifixion with our Lady and St. John on either side. The idea was that one passed out of the nave under the figure of the Crucified Lord into the chancel, where the Risen Lord was in the sacrament on the altar.

At the bottom of the nave was the porch, usually on the south side because of the warmth of the sun. Large porches were important and were often used as schools. All legal matters were conducted here, and also the first part of the sacraments of Baptism, Marriage and Penance. The porch gave onto the churchyard, until comparatively recently without gravestones and therefore used as a place to gather in after a great feast day had been celebrated in church. Because ale was drunk on these occasions, old inns are often very near the church.

In building new churches or when adapting old ones, the nave is one of the most important parts to consider although there is less distinction today between the people's part and the priest's part. One must bear in mind the important principle that people should not only be able to see what is going on but also physically and psychologically be in touch with it. This should dictate the shape of the building more than anything else. A long building makes it difficult, whereas a broad oval-shaped building makes it easy for everybody to see and participate. Each part of the church has to be designed according to its function, so that the physical building reflects the community at worship and assists in a great "sursum corda" — a "lifting up of the heart" towards God.

CONCLUSION

Since I have spoken in this chapter about the church as a physical building, it would be quite easy for us all to miss the simple truth of St. Peter's teaching that the church means essentially the people themselves, as living stones. "Come to Jesus, to that living stone, rejected by men but in God's sight chosen and precious, like living stones by yourselves built into a spiritual house." (I Peter 2: 4 and 5). In these days when church maintenance and appeals have become all important one tends to think of the Church as buildings. Archbishop Ramsay wrote in his book *Canterbury Pilgrim* that: "Indeed Christianity can itself appear to be identified with a particular sort of Western European culture, with its chancels and naves, organs, pews and hassocks but: 'They dreamed not of a perishable home who thus could build' — their vision was in the heavens and the temple of our hearts is more important than a temple of stone."